To Lindsay & Nhat,
Enjoy!!

A TASTE OF SOUTH AFRICA with THE BUTCHER'S WIFE

Kosher

SHARON LURIE

This book is dedicated to two very special ladies in my life: Nanna Jill and Bobba Roch. They left their legacy of love through food. They both ensured that family togetherness was the most important meal of the day and that food nourished the heart so that we'd never be starved of love.

ACKNOWLEDGEMENTS

Without the power and presence of Hashem in every situation, I wouldn't be doing what I'm doing now – acknowledging people in my third book! He has given me the power, the courage and, most certainly, the privilege to be 'The Kosher Butcher's Wife' – the perfect match that enabled me to channel so many of my passions on the road he had mapped for me.

To my husband Ian, my everything. The most positive, loyal, generous, humorous husband ever. However, I have to admit the generosity scale does tilt a bit (in favour of the customer) when I request one of the more popular cuts of meat! But your devotion to your family knows no bounds and your status as 'the biggest mentsch' remains your greatest attribute.

For my Lurie birds

My Son Boruch, also in the family business. Although positive, loyal and generous, you have quickly learnt from your father that in business customers take priority over mommy. But your sense of humour, warmth and kindness overrule any feelings of neglect in the meat department.

My son Darren, my special 'Dumblebee', moved to London where you found your path along the food industry route! Notice a common thread here? I thought your craving for biltong and dry *wors* would tempt you to come home, but that craving merely taught you to make your own British private collection! Your magical presence, exuberance and wholehearted love of family togetherness makes life so much fun.

My son Ryan (aka Jack Sprat, as you won't eat fat) decided as a young boy that you'd rather be a farmer than a butcher, keeping your cattle as super skinny and lean as possible! Your warmth, affection and humour make your intolerance of anything slightly substandard rather helpful when writing a cookery book. It's called taking things with a pinch of salt!

My daughter Eden, also in the family business, your positive, creative, energetic, outgoing personality brings a breath of fresh air to everything you do. Now that I've said all that, I hope you will stop putting my orders at the bottom of the pile. Or will I just have to eat cheese?

For my Lury Jury: To my precious daughters-in-law Rochi, Kim and Hannah and my 'favourite' son-in-law Saul. I thank Hashem every day for blessing my children with their perfect match. Layla, Zahara and Ari, my most treasured and loved grandchildren, when you are in the kitchen with me, creating your own magic in my pots and in my heart – that is when I know I've learnt more about love and life than any recipe could have taught me.

For my creative team and family: My brothers Rod, Graham and Michael, sisters-in-law Steph and Lauren, and all their wonderful children: the laughter, the love and the time we spend together is never enough! To my American family for all your love, support and encouragement, now we can show you what South African food is all about! To Monica and Gerti, the ladies who ensure that my 'test' kitchen is always ready for fun, no matter the time of day!

To my publishing team at Struik Lifestyle from Penguin Random House, Linda de Villiers, Beverley Dodd and Cecilia Barfield. You make the publishing journey so super smooth and enjoyable. Thank you for giving me the opportunity to go round three!

And finally, thank you to you dear readers; it is your support and encouragement that have given me the opportunity to share the recipes in this book with the rest of the world.

Published in 2019 by Struik Lifestyle, an imprint of Penguin Random House South Africa (Pty) Ltd
Company Reg. No. 1953/000441/07
The Estuaries, 4 Oxbow Crescent, Century Avenue, Century City 7441
PO Box 1144, Cape Town, 8000, South Africa

www.penguinrandomhouse.co.za

Reproduction: Hirt & Carter Cape (Pty) Ltd
Printing and binding: RR Donnelley Asia Printing Solutions Ltd

PUBLISHER: Linda de Villiers
DESIGN MANAGER: Beverley Dodd
EDITOR AND INDEXER: Cecilia Barfield
PROOFREADER: Bronwen Maynier
PHOTOGRAPHER: the redhead's studio – Michael Smith
FOOD STYLIST: Lynn Woodward

ISBN 978-1-43230-975-6

CONTENTS

INTRODUCTION

South African cuisine is as deliciously diverse as its people. Ours is an endlessly fascinating epicurean inheritance. Hunter-gatherer herbal infusions and indigenous foraged foods fold into the fermented glories of amasi sour milk from Nguni cattle kraals. Waves of European and Asian settlement are made manifest in Cape Malay clove-and-tamarind-rich delicacies, Afrikaner syrup-laden sweet treats and the fiery feasts of the Durban Indian diaspora. Peri-peri provides tantalising Afro-Lusitanian influences.

South African Jewish cuisine is an exciting element within this magnificent melange. Evolved to honour the spirit and splendour of universal Jewish religious dietary laws, it has become seasoned with the landscapes, climatic conditions and cultural connections of a uniquely African identity. Wherever you are in the world, may you always enjoy the tales and tastes of your home, your heritage, your traditions and your culture.

The recipes that follow make it clear that cooking kosher and being a South African are not mutually exclusive. Rather, from bunny chow, through boerewors, to *tshotlô* and *shisa nyama*, KoshAfrica (African kosher) can – and should be – a proudly South African pleasure …

Cooking Notes

- Vegetables should always be peeled, unless otherwise indicated.
- Use parev chicken stock powder.

Conversion tables

Metric	US cups
5 ml	1 tsp
15 ml	1 Tbsp
60 ml	4 Tbsp or ¼ cup
80 ml	⅓ cup
125 ml	½ cup
160 ml	⅔ cup
200 ml	¾ cup
250 ml	1 cup

OVEN TEMPERATURES

Celsius (°C)	Fahrenheit (°F)	Gas mark
100 °C	200 °F	¼
110 °C	225 °F	¼
120 °C	250 °F	½
140 °C	275 °F	1
150 °C	300 °F	2
160 °C	325 °F	3
180 °C	350 °F	4
190 °C	375 °F	5
200 °C	400 °F	6
220 °C	425 °F	7
230 °C	450 °F	8
240 °C	475 °F	9

BEEFING UP BREAKFASTS

I asked my family what they regarded as a typical South African or their own favourite breakfast. My eldest son answered: ‘Boerewors, pap, tomato, onion and eggs.’ My second eldest son said, ‘Meaty! I’m the butcher’s son, so sausages with hash browns, eggs sunnyside up, macon, sour dough rye, baked beans and avocado – something to keep me going until dinnertime.’ My youngest son agreed, ‘All of the above plus those macon cups from your first book, Ma, they’re the best!’ My daughter shook her head: ‘No question, eggy bread, without a doubt!’ And my husband, loyal as ever to my mother (OBM), said: ‘Nana’s stewed fruit, nothing better!’ And as for me, well it’s a cup of rooibos tea and a homemade rusk!

However, ask the majority of South Africans what their favourite breakfast is and they’ll probably say ‘*umphokoqo*’, which is maize meal cooked to a crumble and covered with amasi or maas (fermented milk in a calabash that could almost be compared to cream cheese or plain yoghurt). The thick liquid is poured over the crumbled maize meal porridge commonly known as *pap*. This was Nelson Mandela’s favourite meal and he could tell if the maas was fermented one day too early or one too late. As they say, you can swap the rural life for an urban environment, but your roots will never leave you.

I’m sure you’ll find your favourites and something special among the recipes that follow.

A Sunday morning surprise when you have challah left over from the day before!

Eggy Bread CHALLAH

1 challah bread
1 tsp ground cinnamon
100g pecan nuts (crushed)
½ cup jam (whatever your favourite is)
3 jumbo eggs
½ cup milk or non-dairy creamer
125g butter (divided into 4)
½ cup syrup

Slice a piece of challah bread, about 1.5cm thick, but not all the way through; stop approximately 1cm from the bottom. Cut the next slice all the way through, so that you have 2 slices of bread joined together at the base. Repeat until you have 4 double slices.

In a bowl, combine the cinnamon, crushed nuts and jam, then spread it generously between each set of slices.

Beat the eggs and milk and dip the stuffed slices of challah into the mixture, making sure both sides are well coated with the egg mixture.

Fry each sandwich in a portion of butter over a medium heat until golden-brown. Remove carefully from the frying pan and drizzle with syrup. Slice into triangles and serve.

There are so many spreading options for stuffed challah: raisins, bananas, blueberries, chocolate spread, peanut butter and jelly ... the list is endless. You could even try cream cheese spread on either side of the bread before dipping in the egg (as pictured here).

MAKES: 4 BUTTERFLIED PIECES OF FRENCH TOAST

GOING NUTS GRANOLA (with a gluten-free option)

1 cup roughly chopped cashew nuts
1 cup roughly chopped hazel or pecan nuts
½ cup slivered almonds
1 cup desiccated coconut
1 cup rolled oats OR cooked quinoa (as a gluten-free substitute)
3 Tbsp melted coconut oil
¼ cup honey (possibly a little extra)
¼ cup brown sugar
a pinch salt
1 cup dried cranberries (optional)

Preheat the oven to 160°C.

Combine all of the ingredients, except the cranberries or raisins, until well mixed and coated. Spread onto a baking tray and shake the tray to space the ingredients more or less evenly. Bake for about 40 minutes or until golden-brown. I usually remove the granola from the oven after 20 minutes, toss it a bit so that it doesn't all clump together, and return to the oven to continue baking.

Once toasted to the perfect crunch, toss and then allow to cool. Add the cranberries (if using) and shake once more. Store in an airtight container.

MAKES: 1–1.5KG

Sorghum (mabele meal as it's also known) is an ancient, African cereal grain. All sorghum is gluten free with a low glycaemic index (GI) and low glycaemic load (GL). It really is an under-appreciated grain; if you're looking for a breakfast that will keep you going until dinnertime, this is probably it.

Always on the hunt for gluten-free recipes, I found this one to be a hit not only as a porridge. but as flapjacks too. It was a real 'flashback' moment, because this is the porridge my coeliac baby lived on, whether with added apple sauce, peanut butter or chicken soup. So when my grandchildren slept over one Saturday night and woke me up at 6am on a cold winter's morning begging for crumpets, I had an instant flashback to 34 years earlier and gave them their dad's favourite porridge, but in flapjack form with banana-cinnamon syrup. They enjoyed them, but said Daisy's crumpets at the shul brocha were better!

MABELE FLASHBACK FLAPJACKS
with peanut butter & banana-cinnamon syrup

---

1 cup fine sorghum meal (e.g. King Korn)
½ cup crushed pecan nuts
1 tsp bicarbonate of soda
1 Tbsp brown sugar
a pinch salt
⅓ cup toasted coconut (optional)
1 cup seedless raisins (optional)
1 x 400ml can coconut milk
6 heaped Tbsp peanut butter, softened in a microwave or in a pot over boiling water, or 250g cream cheese

Banana-cinnamon syrup
2 Tbsp lemon juice
3 ripe (or slightly overripe) bananas, sliced 1cm thick
2 Tbsp butter or non-dairy margarine
1 tsp ground cinnamon
½ cup treacle syrup

To make the flapjacks, combine all the dry ingredients in one bowl and the wet ingredients in another (but keep some of the peanut butter aside for spreading later). Pour the wet mixture into the dry and mix well.

Lightly grease a frying pan with olive oil spray and heat to a medium heat. Drop a quarter cup of batter into the pan and spread out lightly with the back of a spoon. Wait until bubbles form on the top and the mixture no longer looks raw. Ensure that the flapjack is cooked all the way through before turning it over otherwise it may crack or crumble. It will probably need 3 minutes per side. Repeat with the remaining batter. As each flapjack is complete, smear it with peanut butter or cream cheese and spoon over the banana-cinnamon syrup.

For the banana-cinnamon syrup, sprinkle the lemon juice over the banana rings, then fry them in a pan over a medium heat in butter or margarine. Add the cinnamon and syrup and stir carefully.

MAKES: 6–8

This one-skillet dish of eggs poached in a spicy, harissa-infused tomato sauce is one of my daughter Eden's favourite meals. Actually a North African dish that was taken to Israel by Jewish immigrants, it can be served for breakfast, dinner or any time in between. There are a number of versions, but I am sharing a meat recipe. Another version replaces the tomato sauce with a rich spinach and cream sauce loaded with green vegetables and cheese. For convenience, the tomato sauce may be prepared up to 2 days before serving.

Shakshuka is traditionally prepared in a cast iron pan (although most pans will do the trick), but make sure it's clean and presentable, as it should be served straight from the pan for all to enjoy.

SHAKSAUSAGE on mealie meal toast

1 cup mealie meal or polenta (cooked as per packet instructions)
olive oil
500g boerewors or Russian sausages or your favourite breakfast sausage, cut into 4–5cm thick slices
6 eggs

Tomato sauce

2 red peppers, halved, deseeded and chopped
2 large onions, chopped
1 tsp crushed garlic
2 Tbsp cooking oil
2 heaped tsp harissa paste
1 Tbsp tomato paste
1 Tbsp brown sugar
½ tsp ground cumin
2 tsp smoked paprika
a pinch cayenne pepper
2 x 400g cans chopped Italian tomatoes
1 Tbsp chopped fresh thyme or ½ tsp dried
1 Tbsp chopped fresh parsley
salt and pepper to taste
1 Tbsp chopped fresh coriander or parsley for sprinkling

Spread the hot mealie meal or polenta over the base of a 10 x 15cm baking tray. Cover and refrigerate. This can be prepared a day in advance.

To make the tomato sauce, fry the peppers, onions and garlic in the oil until soft. Add the harissa paste, tomato paste, sugar, cumin, paprika and cayenne pepper and stir for a minute. Add the chopped tomatoes and bring to the boil, then lower the heat and allow to simmer for 30 minutes until the sauce reduces and thickens. Finally, add the thyme, parsley and salt and pepper.

Remove the mealie meal or polenta from the fridge. Slice into fingers (or triangles), lightly oil a grilling pan, brush each side of the fingers with olive oil and pan-sear until golden-brown (3–5 minutes per side), then set aside.

Meanwhile, fry the sliced boerewors or sausage in a large frying pan until lightly browned (don't overcook, just brown for colour). Add the tomato sauce to the sausage and keep it warm over a low heat.

Make 6 openings in the tomato sauce and sausage mixture for the eggs. Crack each egg open into a little bowl and then place each egg into the opening created in the sauce. Continue cooking on the stove top until the egg whites start to form and the yolks are done to your preference (although the yolks should be soft).

Place the seared mealie meal or polenta fingers in the tomato sauce, sprinkle with coriander or parsley and serve immediately.

SERVES 6

Occasionally I wake up in the mood for a different breakfast; something a little more indulgent than my usual fishpaste on low-GI bread. I do accept that breakfast is the most important meal of the day, however, fat-free, sugar-free, taste-free granola that requires a high-pressure hose to ensure that my teeth are grain free before my next meeting, doesn't work for me on a daily basis. No, I want something that tastes amazing, that I can enjoy with a cup of tea and that keeps me feeling full until dinnertime. And something that doesn't need an entire roll of floss to make me cross!

Well, I've found it; it's Gila's Cinnamon Roll Cake, which her husband Mendy swears works even better made gluten free! This recipe isn't, but you can substitute cake flour with gluten-free cake mix if you like. A good day to have it is normally a Friday morning. That way I know that it will last me until Shabbos dinner. Ooooh boy, is this good, and if there's any left over, serve it for breakfast on Shabbos.

Gila's CINNAMON ROLL CAKE

3 cups cake flour, sifted
¼ tsp salt
1 cup white sugar
4 tsp baking powder
1½ cups milk
2 eggs
2 tsp vanilla extract
½ cup melted butter

Topping
1 cup butter, softened
1 cup brown sugar
2 Tbsp cake flour, sifted
1 tsp ground cinnamon

Glaze
2 cups icing sugar, sifted
5 Tbsp milk
1 tsp vanilla extract

Preheat the oven to 180°C. Grease a 20 x 30cm baking tin.

Place the 3 cups of flour, salt, sugar, baking powder, milk, eggs and vanilla extract into the bowl of a mixer and mix. Once well combined, add the melted butter and pour into the prepared baking tin.

To make the topping, cream the butter, sugar, flour and cinnamon in a bowl until well combined. Drop evenly over the batter already in the baking tin, then use a knife to marble through the cake batter. Bake for 35–40 minutes or until a toothpick inserted into the middle comes out NEARLY clean.

For the glaze, mix the icing sugar, milk and vanilla together with a whisk in a medium-size bowl. Drizzle evenly over the still-warm cake and serve warm or at room temperature.

SERVES 8–10

My mother was famous for her vanilla and cinnamon tea compote with yoghurt and brûlée topping. It was so delicious that it became known as 'Jill's bestest break'fast' (breaking of the fast) on Yom Kippur (Day of Atonement). Not only is it delicious, but healthy and comforting too. There is always some in our fridge.

VANILLA AND CINNAMON TEA COMPOTE
with yoghurt & brûlée topping

2 vanilla-flavoured tea bags (e.g. Twinings)
1 apple, cinnamon and raisin tea bag (e.g. Twinings)
2 cups boiling water
1kg assorted dried fruit (your favourites)
2 heaped tsp custard powder
4 cups cranberry or pomegranate juice
2 cups full-cream Greek yoghurt
¼ cup brown sugar

Allow the tea bags to draw in the boiling water. Squeeze the bags to ensure maximum flavours are released, then discard the bags.

Place the fruit in a large saucepan and cover with the brewed tea. Bring to the boil, then turn down the heat to low and simmer for 30 minutes.

Mix the custard powder in the cranberry or pomegranate juice, then add to the fruit. Allow to simmer for a few minutes until the sauce thickens slightly. Don't stir too much as the fruit will break up. Remove from the heat and leave to cool.

Once cool, cover the fruit mixture with the yoghurt and sprinkle over the sugar. Either brûlée with a blow torch or place under the griller until golden-brown and bubbling.

SERVES 8

LET'S ZOOP IT UP

I wrote this chapter on the coldest day of the year.
Snow in South Africa? No, that wouldn't occur!
But a fire with logs, now that's something I'd love
With bean and barley soup, I could never tire of.
However, for me, I can eat in any season
So cold weather today is certainly not a reason.
Some of these recipes can be enjoyed as a meal
So hearty and nutritious, just part of the deal
A ladle of love in every bowl
What more do you need to nourish your soul?

I come from Durban, from the Kingdom of KwaZulu-Natal, and as a little girl I ate madumbis, so I get very excited when I see them. They are a root vegetable and, for the purposes of this recipe, could be compared to a taro root, yam, sweet potato or regular potato. This soup is similar to a leek and potato soup, so if you're unable to find madumbis, use a combination of potatoes or your favourite potatoes.

MADUMBI SOUP

2 onions, chopped
6 leeks, sliced
canola oil for frying
1 tsp crushed fresh garlic
1 celeriac bulb, cubed
2 turnips, cubed
500g large white sweet potatoes, cubed
500g large potatoes, cubed
500g madumbis, cubed
2 litres water (maybe a little extra)
3 Tbsp chicken stock powder
3 Tbsp onion soup powder
3 cubes vegetable stock
3 cups boiling water
1 cup non-dairy creamer
salt and pepper to taste
250g pastrami, shredded

Fry the onions and leeks in a little oil until softened. Add the garlic, celeriac, turnips, sweet potatoes, potatoes, madumbis and water (the water must cover the vegetables). Bring to the boil, then allow to simmer for 2–3 hours.

Dissolve all the stock and soup powder in the boiling water, add to the vegetable mix and allow to simmer for another 20–30 minutes. Finally, add the non-dairy creamer and blend together until smooth with a hand blender or in a liquidiser or food processor. Check the seasoning and adjust where necessary.

Fry the pastrami, allow to cool and then sprinkle over the soup when ready to serve.

If you'd prefer a dairy version of the soup, use regular dairy cream instead of non-dairy creamer, and sprinkle over crumbled feta or grated cheese just before serving, instead of the pastrami.

SERVES 8–10

In the 17th century, the Dutch East India Company needed a refreshment station for ships travelling from Europe to the East. Dutch settlers landed at the Cape with orders to establish farms to provide fresh vegetables and meat for the ships rounding the Cape of Good Hope. And so, Dutch and Southeast Asian cuisine had a significant influence on South African food. I need a refreshment station every time I travel around a shopping mall, so I don't think the Dutch were asking for too much!

DUTCH PEA AND CASHEW NUT SOUP

2 large onions, roughly chopped
3 stalks celery
3 Tbsp canola oil
1kg frozen peas
2 litres water
2 large potatoes, sliced
1 bunch spinach, roughly chopped
1 cup raw cashew nuts
2 bay leaves
¼ cup chicken stock powder
3 Tbsp finely chopped fresh basil
¼ cup finely chopped fresh mint
1 tsp salt
freshly ground black pepper to taste

Fry the onions and celery in the oil until soft. Add the peas, water, potatoes, spinach, cashew nuts and bay leaves and bring to the boil. Cover and simmer for 1½–2 hours over a low heat until the vegetables are very soft, then remove the bay leaves.

Add the chicken stock powder, basil, mint, salt and pepper and stir well. Blend the soup until smooth with an immersion or stick blender.

Serve hot with crusty bread.

SERVES 10–12

There I was standing in this huge supermarket in Dallas, USA. Alone and a little flustered, overwhelmed at not knowing where to start. I had my list of ingredients, but that didn't help much. I wanted to make my family a soup with a Mex-African fusion. Searching for cumin alone took me up and down 33 aisles! But I loved it too. I felt like a child let loose in a candy store; there were so many exciting products.

Of course, I got home to: 'Who chops fresh onions and carrots? You can get that in the freezer section.' But I wanted a homemade soup, packed with the freshest of ingredients, nutrients and love that no pre-made carton of soup could give them. All that was left to do after painfully grating, chopping, hulling and watching it simmer for a couple of hours was to cool, blend and pack it into Ziploc bags, ready for the freezer. But enter the 'klutz'.

I placed the 2-gallon (yes, it's gallons in the US) Ziploc bag in the sink and started pouring the soup. Happy that it was three-quarters full and feeling good that my sister-in-law had one less course to prepare for Yomtov, I carefully sealed the bag and confidently lifted it to put into the nearby freezer. It was heavy-ish as I lifted it and turned away from the sink, but not as heavy as my heart when I heard the horrific sound of soup slapping the tiled floor and escaping under the fridge to its final hiding place. Standing there, drenched in carrots from the waist down, I was the ultimate picture of a 'flustered klutz'. There was no trace of carrot after my four-hour clean up and suddenly those cartons of store-bought soup became incredibly attractive!

Carrots are a goldmine of nutrients. For the best taste results, use fresh all the way – you can definitely taste the difference between fresh and anything frozen or precut.

Flustered Klutz
CARROT AND SPICY CHICKPEA SOUP

---

3 Tbsp oil
2 onions, roughly chopped
1kg carrots, roughly chopped
1 Tbsp brown sugar
1 Tbsp finely grated fresh ginger
2 tsp ground cumin
2 tsp hot curry powder
2 x 400g cans chickpeas (retain ½ cup for decorating)
2 tsp chopped fresh red chillies or 1 tsp dried chilli flakes
4 cups water
3 cups homemade chicken stock or 3 stock cubes dissolved in 3 cups water
3 bay leaves
½ cup techina (optional)

Heat the oil in a large soup pot and fry the onions and carrots, stirring all the time to keep them well coated with the oil. Add the sugar and continue cooking until the sugar has dissolved. Stir for 5–10 minutes until the carrots and onions start to caramelise and the edges turn slightly brown.

Add the ginger, cumin, curry powder, chickpeas, all the chickpea liquid, chillies, water, chicken stock and bay leaves. Bring to the boil, then reduce the heat and allow to simmer, covered, for 1 hour until the vegetables are tender.

Meanwhile, fry the retained chickpeas in a little oil until crispy. Remove from the heat and drain on kitchen paper.

Discard the bay leaves from the soup, then liquidise until smooth. If you prefer it less thick, add a little water.

Sprinkle the fried chickpeas over the soup. If you are using techina, add a little water to give it the consistency of pouring cream, then swirl it into the soup. It gives the soup a lovely light and tasty lift.

SERVES 8–10

This green vegetable soup is a delicious way to enjoy greens that are so important in the diet. Vegetables contain an array of antioxidants and other disease-fighting compounds. Some plant chemicals can reduce inflammation and eliminate possible carcinogens.

Just as chicken soup is known as *bobba*'s (granny's) penicillin, so this soup is the heartiest and most beneficial for a vegetarian. But should you wish to make more of a meal out of the soup, add some barley, or to keep it gluten free, samp, beans and lentils will do the trick.

GROEN GROENTESOP (souper-greens soup)

3 large onions, chopped
3 stalks celery, chopped
2 leeks, chopped
3 Tbsp olive oil
2 litres water
3 large potatoes, cubed
250g tender-stem broccoli, chopped
3 large courgettes (baby marrows), sliced
400g shredded green cabbage
100g baby spinach
250g frozen petit pois
200g green beans, chopped
35g fresh parsley, chopped
1 Tbsp chopped fresh thyme or 1 tsp dried
¼ cup powdered vegetable stock
¼ cup powdered onion stock
salt and pepper to taste

Fry the onions, celery and leeks in the oil until soft. Add the water, potatoes, broccoli, courgettes, cabbage, spinach, petit pois, green beans and parsley. Bring to the boil, then reduce the heat and allow to simmer for 2 hours. Finally, add the thyme, vegetable stock, onion stock and seasoning. Stir well to ensure the stock powders dissolve properly. Stock powders should only be added once the vegetables are cooked, because the thickeners in the powders slow down the vegetable cooking process.

Blend the soup in a food processor by pulsing it a few times; not too smoothly, as it should have some texture. I find it easiest to use an immersion or stick blender to achieve the desired consistency. Check for seasoning once more, just before serving. Remember, salt brings out the flavour in any dish.

SERVES 10–12

My nephew Ethan begged me recently for broccoli and cheese soup. 'You haven't made it in a while!' he pleaded. He was right; I last made it one Shavuot. Who can ignore a special nephew, so I searched for the recipe (which I received from a friend in America), and here it is.

BROCCOLI AND CHEESE SOUP
with feta & onion challah (dairy recipe)

2 large onions, chopped
2 Tbsp butter
salt to taste
2 cloves garlic, crushed
500–600g broccoli stems*
2 Tbsp cake flour
3 heaped Tbsp vegetable stock powder dissolved in 3 cups boiling water
2 cups full-cream milk
1 cup thick cream
250g cream cheese
3 cups grated Cheddar cheese
½ tsp grated nutmeg
pepper to taste

Feta and onion challah

1 onion, sliced into rings
cooking oil
1 egg, beaten
1 x quantity challah dough (page 48)
a handful crumbled feta

Fry the onions in the butter until limp, add salt and the garlic, stir for a minute, then add the broccoli. Sprinkle with the flour and continue to fry over a medium heat for 4–5 minutes, but don't allow the broccoli to turn brown.

Add the vegetable stock, bring to the boil, reduce the heat and allow to simmer for about 30 minutes, until the broccoli starts to break up when pressed with a fork. Remove from the heat, add the milk, cream and cream cheese and mix well. Return to the heat and gradually add the grated cheese, allowing it to melt into the soup, which should have a lovely thick, velvety smoothness with threads of broccoli running through it.

Finally, add the nutmeg, check for salt and pepper and serve with feta and onion challah.

To make a feta and onion challah, lightly fry the onion rings in oil until soft but not brown. After egg washing a homemade, plaited challah dough, place the onions and the crumbled feta over the top of the dough. Bake as you would normally bake a challah bread (30–35 minutes). This can also be done with par-baked challahs available from most supermarkets: egg wash, add onion and feta and bake as per instructions.

*Some stores' broccoli have extra-long stems. For kashrut reasons, I cut off the bushy tops, check the stems for tunnelling and chop them into 3cm slices. If you can find kosher frozen broccoli, use that instead.

SERVES 8–10

This is the quickest spicy lentil, sweetcorn and butternut soup you'll ever make.

YENTIL SOUP
with an African twist or two (or three)

1kg butternut, cubed
2 large potatoes, cubed
water
2 x 400g cans lentils
2 x 410g cans whole kernel corn
1 tsp harissa spice
1 tsp curry powder
3 Tbsp vegetable stock powder
1 x 165ml can coconut cream
salt and pepper to taste
finely chopped fresh coriander for serving

Soup toppings
½ cup toasted sunflower seeds
½ cup crunchy toasted corn
a pinch dukkah spice

Add the butternut and potatoes to a saucepan. Pour in sufficient water to cover by 5cm, bring to the boil and cook until soft. Blend with a hand blender or food processor until smooth.

Add the lentils, corn, harissa spice, curry powder, vegetable stock and coconut cream and bring to the boil. Reduce the heat and allow to simmer for 30 minutes with the lid lying loosely on top. Switch off the heat, replace the lid firmly and allow the soup to absorb all the wonderful flavours. Check the seasoning, as lentils love salt.

Sprinkle with the coriander and a topping of your choice (or all of them) before serving.

SERVES 8–10

CHALLA-VALOT BREAD SPOT

If you offered me a scone, it's notforme.com
If you tempted me with cheesecake, for that I'd stay awake
If you suggested a croissant, I may act nonchalant
If you gave me a pastry, my reverse would be hasty
But if you gave me a baguette, a challah or a bagel
You may never get me away from your dinner table
I have to admit my weakness is bread
Especially with biltong. That's me fed.

I first tasted these crackers at a friend's *simcha* (celebration) and didn't realise they were banting, shmanting, sugar free, dairy free, gluten free and I know what you're thinking, taste free too.

But no, they are really delicious and I can't make enough of them. My family eats them with almost everything; whether with chopped liver, chopped herring, snoek pâté or crumbled on a salad, they're a winner. The biggest win of all was when a family member who works for my hero, Yotam Ottolenghi, visited South Africa and said, 'OMG, I have to take some of these back for Yotam to try – we need to make them.' *Halevei* (if only)!

The Ultimate HEALTH CRACKERS

2 Tbsp psyllium husks
2 Tbsp chia seeds
2 cups water
600g seeds of your choice (e.g. sunflower, sesame, linseed)
1 tsp salt
1 tsp garlic salt
¼ tsp cayenne pepper
3 Tbsp melted coconut oil

Preheat the oven to 170°C. Line 2 medium, rectangular baking trays with silicone sheets or baking paper.

Mix the psyllium husks, chia seeds and water. Set aside for 5 minutes until it has a gel-like consistency. Add the rest of the ingredients and mix thoroughly. Set aside for 1 hour.

Spread the mixture thinly over the base of the prepared trays. Bake for approximately 40 minutes. Remove from the oven, break or cut into crackers and return to the oven to crisp for another 10–15 minutes. Remove from the oven, but if you feel they still need more crisping, return to the oven for a further 10–15 minutes.

Once out of the oven, peel off the baking paper and leave to cool. Store in an airtight container. Eat as a snack or serve with toppings such as cream cheese, tomato, herb pesto, hummus or avocado. *Es gezunterheit* (may you eat them in good health).

MAKES 40–50 (DEPENDING HOW LARGE OR SMALL THEY ARE CUT)

This bun found its way into South African cuisine courtesy of the French Huguenots who settled in Franschhoek in the Cape. Just as they contributed so significantly to the development of viticulture in the region, they also brought their cooking and baking traditions with them. *Mosbolletjies* were made during the wine-making season when unfermented grape juice (stum) was readily available. Afrikaans for 'stum' or 'must' is '*mos*', and '*bolletjies*' is the Afrikaans word for 'little balls or buns'.

As a bread lover, I simply had to include a *mossbolletjie* recipe, but I've replaced grape juice with rooibos tea. If you don't finish the *babke* (served hot with lashings of butter), you could dry them to make rusks to serve with tea or coffee.

MOSSBOLLETJIE ROOIBOS BABKE

4 cups cake flour
2 tsp salt
½ cup white sugar
10g rapid rising dried yeast
2 cups rooibos tea, made from 1 tea bag
125g butter or margarine
1 cup warm water
1 cup milk or soya milk, room temperature
¾ cup apricot jam
½ cup brown sugar mixed with 1 Tbsp ground cinnamon
1 cup raisins or sultanas, or a mixture of both (optional)
2 eggs

Sift the flour and salt together in a bowl. Add the white sugar and yeast and mix well.

Once the tea has steeped for 2–3 minutes, squeeze the bag to extract maximum flavour. Place the hot tea into a bowl, then add the butter or margarine, warm water and milk. As soon as the butter has melted, add the liquid mixture to the dry ingredients. Knead the resulting dough well until smooth and elastic, then place into an oiled bowl, cover with clingfilm and leave to prove until doubled in size (30–40 minutes).

Knock back the dough, then roll out until it is about 2cm thick. Smear with the apricot jam and sugar-cinnamon, and sprinkle over the raisins or sultanas, if using. Divide the dough into 8–10 equal pieces. Roll each piece into a rounded oblong and pack them tightly together into a greased loaf tin. Cover and allow to prove for another 30 minutes.

Preheat the oven to 180°C.

Beat the eggs and brush over the top of the loaf. Bake for 35–40 minutes until golden and risen. Leave to cool on a wire rack.

MAKES 1 LOAF

This is a wonderful, last-minute flatbread to make when you're not sure if your tea guests are going to become drink or dinner guests! It can be served alongside anything you may have in your cupboard: canned asparagus, pickled cucumbers, pickled onions, olives, salsa, a couple of dips, cut up fresh vegetables, some pretzels, nuts and crisps.

PASTRAMI AND OLIVE CORNMEAL FLATBREAD

¼ cup olive oil for greasing the pans
250g pastrami or macon, sliced
oil for frying
1½ cups cornmeal or polenta
½ cup bread or gluten-free bread flour
2 tsp white sugar
1 tsp bicarbonate of soda
½ tsp salt
1¾ cups soya milk
2 eggs
1 tsp dried mixed herbs
2 Tbsp olive oil
½ cup sundried tomatoes in oil, drained and chopped (e.g. Woolworths sundried tomato quarters)
16 pitted olives, roughly chopped
1 small onion, halved and thinly sliced
1 cup thinly sliced mushrooms
needles from sprigs of fresh rosemary

Preheat the oven to 190°C. Grease 2 round cake tins with a diameter of 20–22cm or an equivalent baking tray with the olive oil.

Fry the pastrami or macon in a little oil.

In a bowl, combine the cornmeal or polenta, flour, sugar, bicarbonate of soda and salt. In another bowl, combine the soya milk with the eggs, dried herbs and 2 tablespoons of olive oil. Add the wet ingredients to the dry ingredients and mix together. Fold in the pastrami or macon, sundried tomatoes and olives.

Heat the prepared tins or tray in the preheated oven for about 5 minutes. Remove from the oven and pour in the batter. Sprinkle with the onion, mushrooms and rosemary needles and bake for 20–25 minutes until golden-brown.

MAKES 2 SMALLER LOAVES OR 1 LARGE LOAF

Roosterkoek (you have to roll those R's!) is the traditional style of bread that accompanies a braai or barbecue. These little breads are prepared by rolling bread dough into flattened balls and cooking them on a grid over the coals. They're best enjoyed piping hot and straight off the grill.

ROOSTERKOEK

500g white bread flour
1 tsp salt
1½ cups lukewarm water
10g rapid rising dried yeast
1 tsp sugar
1 Tbsp olive oil

In a large mixing bowl, mix together the flour and salt. Add the water, yeast and sugar and mix well, then knead by hand until it becomes a smooth dough. Set aside in the bowl with a little olive oil over the top of the bread, and allow the dough to double in size. When ready, knock back the dough and divide into 8 balls.

Roll each ball out on a floured surface. Cover with a warm damp dishcloth or a lightly oiled plastic sheet and leave to rise for another 20 minutes. Dust the tops with more flour and place over low coals. Keep turning the roosterkoek every 3–4 minutes to ensure that they are golden-brown, cooked through and make a hollow sound when you knock them.

MAKES 8

If you were to ask my friends what I could never live without, they would all answer in unison "bread and meat". I love, live and breathe bread. Life is so simple being a meataholic and breadaholic, nothing beats a biltong bagel or a steak wrap. For the extra vitamins there's always multivitamins!

ROTIS

400g cake flour
1 tsp salt
3 Tbsp olive oil
1 cup boiling water

In a medium bowl, sift together the flour and salt. Add the oil and water and mix quickly with a wooden spoon until the dough comes away clean from the sides of the bowl. Turn the dough out onto a well-floured surface. Knead until smooth and pliable (about 5 minutes).

Preheat an unoiled skillet or flat frying pan to a medium-high heat. Divide the dough into 12 equal parts, shape into rounds and cover with a damp cloth. Flatten the balls with the palm of your hand, then use a rolling pin to roll out each into a circle with a diameter of 15–18cm and a thickness of 2–3mm. Lift them up and roll them onto the rolling pin, then unroll them into the skillet or pan.

Cook each roti for 1 minute before turning over, then turn again after another minute. They should have some darker brown spots when ready. Remove them from the pan, roll them up quickly and cover with a clean but slightly damp dishcloth. Cover with the cloth until the next roti is ready to be taken off the heat.

MAKES 12

Oh no! It was another of those load-shedding nights in the middle of winter and I was preparing for a braai (which is a good idea when you don't have electricity). However, I had made up a batch of corn bread and couldn't bake it in the oven without electricity. Suddenly the penny dropped! Why not steam it in a pot over the fire or on a gas stove? And, as you guessed, it was so good I always do it that way now.

Before you begin, make sure you have three cans in which to steam the bread, as well as a large, deep pot to place them in because the boiling water shouldn't splash into the bread. You can use canned mealies (well drained, and retain the liquid), but not the cream-style variety, because that will result in a gooey mess.

Steam-Can MEALIE BREAD

- 2 cups yellow mealies, frozen or canned
- 2 cups white bread flour
- 2 Tbsp sugar
- 4 tsp baking powder
- 1 tsp salt
- 2 cups liquid (from canned mealies if using) or water (if using frozen)

Grease 3 cans well.

Blend the mealies in a food processor, then transfer to a bowl. Mix in the remaining ingredients with enough water to form a stiff dough. Set aside for 10 minutes, then scoop the dough into the prepared cans (it should only reach two-thirds of the way up). Seal each can with 2 sheets of aluminium foil sprayed with oil on the underside so that the bread doesn't stick to it.

Bring a pot of water to the boil for the cans to stand in; the water should reach halfway up the sides of the cans. Insert the cans, cover the pot and reduce to a simmer that still allows visible steam. Steam the cans for 1 hour, but check after 30 minutes in case you need to add more water to the pot.

Serve the bread hot or at room temperature. Either way it is delicious with lashings of butter or non-dairy margarine. I love it hot with pieces of boerewors on top.

MAKES 3 SMALL LOAVES

A couple of years ago some members of our community were participating in a fundraiser – their mission was to climb Mount Kilimanjaro, the highest peak in Africa. I was contacted by a member of this ladies-only team to assist with a recipe. As there wouldn't be ovens for them to make challah for Shabbos, they needed an alternative method for potted bread. I'd never made potted bread before, let alone challah. No doubt this was to be a first for Mount Kilimanjaro.

Part of my radio work obviously includes reviewing recipe books and chatting to the authors. That particular week, and we know nothing happens by chance, I reviewed the book *Ukutya Kwasekhaya: Tastes from Nelson Mandela's Kitchen* written by Xoliswa Ndoyiya, personal chef to the former president. Paging through the book I noticed a recipe for *umbhako* (pot bread). I tried it and to this day it's an absolute winner. No excuses when camping anymore that we can't bake bread! Here's the answer straight from Madiba's kitchen. It's delicious with butter and jam.

Xoliswa Ndoyiya's UMBHAKO (POT BREAD) CHALLAH

---

2 Tbsp butter or margarine
6 cups cake flour
1½ tsp salt
1 tsp sugar
10g rapid rising dried yeast
lukewarm water as needed

You will need a 2-litre cast iron pot with a tight-fitting lid. Using the butter or margarine, generously grease the inside of both the pot and the lid.

Sieve the flour and salt into a bowl and mix in the sugar and yeast. Gradually add enough warm water to form a dough. The amount will vary according to the humidity in the air. Knead until firm but elastic. Place the dough in a lightly oiled bowl, cover with a damp cloth and set aside in a warm spot until doubled in size (about 1 hour).

Knock down the dough and knead again, then roll it into a ball and place in the prepared pot. Cover with the lid and set aside until the dough has once more doubled in size. Once the dough has risen almost to the top of the pot, put the pot on the stove over a low heat and cook, covered, until the bread has set (about 30 minutes).

Take the bread out of the pot, turn it over, return to the pot, cover and cook for another 30 minutes so that the bread has a golden-brown crust on the top and the bottom.

Traditionally this bread is made over a fire. If you make it over a fire, place some coals on top of the pot lid so that the bread cooks evenly on all sides.

MAKES 1 LARGE POT-SHAPED LOAF

This loaf can also be cooked in a heavy-based pot as described in the previous recipe.

The Kosher Butcher's Wife's
OVEN CHALLAH

1 cup warm water
8 cups cake flour
2 x 10g sachets dried yeast (e.g. Anchor)
¾ cup sugar
4 tsp salt
¾ cup oil
2 cups warm water
2 eggs plus 1 extra for glazing

Place all the ingredients (except the egg for glazing), in the order listed, into the bowl of a food processor with a dough hook. On the lowest speed, mix until all the ingredients are combined, then increase the speed slightly and continue kneading until the mixture turns into a nice, well-blended ball of dough. You may need to add a little more water if the dough is too firm, or a little more flour if the dough is still sticking to the sides of the bowl. I prefer the dough to be slightly more moist, as the air tends to dry it out during the hand kneading stage.

Remove the dough from the machine and start kneading by hand. If the dough sticks to your hands, sprinkle a little flour on the table. Knead for about 5 minutes and use the special time for yourself, your challahs and Hashem.

Once the dough is soft and smooth, leave it to rise for 1–2 hours until doubled in size. Knock down and divide into 3 or 4 equal portions (depending on how large you prefer the challah). Plait as desired and place on a baking tray or in a loaf tin. Leave to rise again until doubled in size.

Preheat the oven to 180°C.

When ready, paint the challah with egg wash (1 egg mixed with 2 tablespoons of water) and bake for 30–35 minutes until golden-brown. So easy, so simple and so fulfilling!

MAKES 1 LOAF

‘When the sauce of stew goes into these dumplings, that’s the best!’ says Xoliswa Ndoyiya. These best-ever dumplings are courtesy of Xoliswa – Nelson Mandela’s private chef.

DOMBOLO (dumplings)

600g cake flour
1 tsp salt
1 tsp sugar
10g dried yeast
2½ cups lukewarm water
2 Tbsp butter or oil

Sieve the flour and salt into a bowl and mix in the sugar and yeast. Gradually add the lukewarm water, mixing until a soft dough forms.

Knead the dough until it is smooth and elastic, then cover the bowl with clingfilm and set aside in a warm place until doubled in size (about 1 hour).

Melt the butter or oil in a large cast iron pot. Roll the dough into balls the size of your palm. Place the balls in the melted butter or oil and pour boiling water into the pot to a depth of 2cm. Cover and cook over a medium heat until the dumplings are cooked through (about 20 minutes). As the water evaporates the butter or oil will begin to fry the base of the dumplings. Keep an eye on them to check that they don’t burn and add a little more water if necessary.

Serve hot with a meat dish such as *umleqwa* (chicken stew).

MAKES 3

My cousin Brenda is a true perfectionist in the art of ‘no-knead’ health bread. Make this once and I promise, there’ll be no-knead to buy a loaf ever again. The only thing you will knead, is to make it again and again.

Brenda’s AMASI BREAD

4 cups nutty wheat flour
1 tsp bicarbonate of soda
1 tsp baking powder
1 tsp salt
3 Tbsp honey
2 cups plain yoghurt or amasi
½ cup sunflower oil
¼ cup milk
½ cup mixed seeds (sesame, sunflower, poppy, etc) (optional)

Preheat the oven to 180°C. Grease a loaf tin.

In a bowl, combine the flour, bicarbonate of soda, baking powder and salt. Mix in the honey. Stir in the yoghurt or amasi, oil and milk until all is well mixed, followed by the seeds if using. Spoon into the prepared tin and bake for 45 minutes. Reduce the heat to 160°C, remove the loaf from the tin, turn it over so that the top is on the base of the tin, then return to the oven and bake for a further 15 minutes.

MAKES 1 LOAF

LET'S MEAT AND EAT

Meat is generally a big part of the South African diet and is hardly ever left out of a meal. As with kosher meat, cheaper cuts are used to create exceptional meals. With the wonderful smorgasbord of meats available, I'm sure many recipes here will become favourites.

They say … if you want to be energetic, calm and wise, there's only one solution – eat *inyama* (the isiZulu word for 'meat'). Who am I to argue with the experts?

Meat is a nutritional one-stop health shop as it is a source of iron, zinc, vitamins, calcium, and amino and omega acids, to name but a few. Throw in its ability to aid digestion, help control blood sugar levels and prevent muscle loss. It will also assist in keeping you in shape, because it reduces cravings for unhealthy foods and leaves you feeling fuller for longer. All this and full of energy too! Now there's something for you to sink your teeth into!

And speaking of teeth, have you ever tried to take a piece of well-chewed biltong away from a teething baby? A scream that will frighten you to the very core! Our teeth and stomachs are designed to digest meat and our senses to stimulate hunger. Are you able to walk past a burger or boerewors braai and not be seduced by the incredible aroma that wafts through the air? It will press that hunger button immediately! After all, who can resist the sizzle of a burger, chop or steak as it's slapped onto smoking and shimmering heat, or the tantalising aroma of flame-licked meat emblazoned with a dark brown crust?

What a thrilling way to nourish our bodies. Seems senseless not to try a piece of meat off the braai.

Essen, fressen, it's my favourite obsession!

BEEF

Keeping kosher often makes self-catering a little challenging, especially when you're away over Shabbos. However, a crockpot may be one of the best appliances you'll ever find room for in your car. Leave the kitchen sink, but don't forget to take the crockpot. In fact, you can use it for almost any meal. There is nothing better than returning from a day of animal spotting to a meal that's hot, delicious and perfect. This is just one of my favourite crockpot meals. Who would have imagined hot beef on rye on a cold night in the African bush, or a delicious curry that's been simmering all day?

Bushy-Eyed HONEY-MUSTARD BRISKET

2–2.5kg pickled brisket or hump
½ cup honey
½ cup brown treacle sugar
3 Tbsp grainy mustard
¼ cup smooth Dijon mustard
1 cup ginger ale

Wash the pickled brisket or hump very well, as the pickling solution contains quite a bit of salt. Place the meat into the crockpot.

Mix together the honey, sugar, mustards and ginger ale, then pour over the meat and cook on low for at least 8 hours. You need less liquid than you would if you cooked this in the oven. Steam forms in the crockpot and keeps the meat moist. (You'll see the condensation forming on the lid, while the meat also gives off liquid during cooking.)

Slice and serve with mashed potatoes, a garlic and mustard sauce and peas, or serve on rye bread with piccalilli, pickled cucumbers and sauerkraut.

SERVES 8

A stew, and particularly a red stew (*ebomvu* is isiZulu for 'red'), is something you should always have in your freezer. But not like the one I had at a friend's house as a child! The meat was boiled, with unpeeled carrots cut into all sorts of shapes and sizes, and so much water that the hard potatoes weren't sure whether to sink or swim! I almost feel *ibel* (nauseous) at the thought. Stews are all about the colour, so if it means adding Staffords browning sauce, do it!

Konfyt is the Afrikaans word for 'jam'. I have included a recipe for tomato *konfyt* (page 190), which goes so well with many of the meat dishes I make. The fresh ginger root and hot chilli take the edge off too much sweetness.

EBOMVU INYAMA (RED MEAT) STEW with tomato konfyt

- 2kg cubed deboned stewing beef
- 3 large onions, chopped
- 2 cups dry red wine
- 6–8 cloves garlic
- 3 Tbsp powdered beef stock
- 2 cups water
- 2 x 400g cans good quality Italian tomatoes
- 2 Tbsp tomato paste
- 3 Tbsp tomato *konfyt* (page 190 or readymade if you must)
- 1 Tbsp honey or equivalent sweetener
- 4 bay leaves
- salt and pepper to taste

Fry the meat in a large, heavy-based frying pan until brown on all sides. Remove and set aside. In the same frying pan, fry the onions until soft, then add the wine. Cook until the wine reduces and the alcohol cooks out.

Add the garlic, beef stock, water, Italian tomatoes, tomato paste, tomato jam, honey and bay leaves. Return the meat to the pan and bring to the boil. Reduce to a simmer and allow to cook for 1 hour or until the meat is soft. Season to taste.

Everything can also be placed in a roasting dish and cooked in the oven at 160°C for 2 hours.

SERVES 8

Whenever a South African says *jislaaik* (pronounced 'yis-like'), it's normally said with some sort of surprise. For instance in rugby, if a man scores a try by running from one end of the field to the other, avoiding all the other players, that's *jislaaik*. Or if something tastes delicious you say, '*Jislaaik* this is good!'

Jislaaik RIBELICIOUS RIBS

3 racks meaty-smoked steakhouse ribs, cut up individually (± 20 ribs, each ± 12cm long)
2 litres cola
1 tsp crushed fresh garlic
1 heaped Tbsp grated ginger
1 tsp dried chilli flakes

Basting sauce

1 cup tomato sauce (e.g. All Gold) or ketchup
¼ cup hotdog mustard (your favourite)
¼ cup soy sauce
¼ cup smooth apricot jam

Wash the ribs well to remove excess salt from the smoking process. Place them in a large pot and cover with the cola, garlic ginger and chilli flakes. Don't worry if they are not covered completely as there should be sufficient liquid to steam them. Bring to the boil, then reduce the heat to a simmer and allow the ribs to cook for at least 30 minutes. After 15 minutes swap the ribs at the bottom of the pot to the top so that all the ribs are cooked evenly in the cola.

Preheat the oven to 180°C. Transfer the ribs to a roasting dish, discarding any cola that hasn't already cooked out.

To make the basting sauce, mix the tomato sauce or ketchup, mustard, soy sauce and apricot jam in a bowl until well combined. Baste the ribs with this mixture, then roast in the oven, covered, for 1 hour, turning after 30 minutes. After an hour, reduce the heat to 160°C and roast for another hour, uncovered, until the ribs are dark and crispy.

SERVES 6

Cabbage! The minute I hear the word, I think '*holishkes*', although there is so much more to this green leaf than we realise. It is a very traditional vegetable in South African cooking, and grows so well and quickly in most gardens.

Chef, food editor and author Hope Malau, in his book *Johanne 14*, explains the importance of cabbage in South African township life (cabbage being a staple food second only to maize meal in the country), as well as the Biblical origin of its name in townships (from John 14, 'Let not your heart be troubled...'). He says, 'A head of cabbage can be cooked in so many different ways; it is inexpensive and goes with anything ... it will give you a wholesome meal every time. Hence it's now humorously become known as "Johanne 14".'

DECONSTRUCTED SLOPPY JOES or holishkes (cabbage blintzes)

1 whole head green or red cabbage
3 cups boiling water
2 large potatoes, thinly sliced (optional)
vegetable oil for spraying (optional)

Meat mixture

1kg beef mince
½ cup warm water
1 Tbsp chicken soup powder
2 Tbsp onion soup powder
3 Tbsp finely chopped fresh flat-leaf parsley
2 Tbsp tomato paste
2 Tbsp brown sugar
1 Tbsp crushed garlic
2 cups cooked rice
salt and pepper to taste

Sauce

2 x 410g cans Italian-style peeled and chopped tomatoes (with liquid)
2 Tbsp honey or syrup of your choice
1 Tbsp finely grated fresh ginger
1 Tbsp cornflour dissolved in ½ cup cold water
1 Tbsp chicken stock powder
1 Tbsp tomato paste
salt and pepper to taste

Using a sharp knife in a circular motion, carefully remove the hard, white centre core of the cabbage, about 6–8cm down. Separate the leaves, wash well and place them in a large saucepan. Cover with the boiling water and steam the cabbage until soft, then switch off the heat and leave to cool in the covered pan.

Meanwhile, combine the ingredients for the meat mixture until well mixed.

Mix together the sauce ingredients, then blitz in a food processor or with a handheld blender until smooth.

Remove the cooled cabbage from the saucepan. If some leaves have very thick centre veins, cut a small 'V' to remove the thicker part of the vein. Alternatively, roll a rolling pin over the thick part of the cabbage to soften.

Preheat the oven to 180°C. At this point you have two options:

Option 1 (deconstructed sloppy Joes/cabbage and meat casserole): Pour a layer of sauce into a rectangular ovenproof dish, followed by a thin layer of finely crumbled meat mixture. Cover the meat with a layer of cabbage leaves, which can be cut into smaller pieces for easier serving. Ensure that the meat is completely covered by the cabbage. Continue layering in this fashion until sauce and meat are used up. Finally (optional), add a layer of thinly sliced potatoes, spray with a little vegetable oil and bake for about 30 minutes or until the potatoes are soft and golden-brown and the sauce is bubbling.

Option 2 (*holishkes*): Roll 3–4 tablespoons of the meat mixture into a ball. Place the ball in the centre of a cabbage leaf, tuck in the sides and roll up. Don't worry if the 'parcel' isn't perfect. Repeat with the remaining meat and leaves. Pour half of the sauce into a rectangular ovenproof dish and arrange the stuffed cabbage leaves in the sauce, side by side. Cover with the remaining sauce and bake for 35–45 minutes until the sauce thickens and the parcels are golden-brown. Serve with rice or mashed potato.

STAINLESS ROSTFREI INOX

With the sauce as the hero of this dish, the steaks on the bone need very little spicing. Just salt and ground black pepper are the way to go.

PRIME RIB STEAK
& herbichurri sauce

4 prime rib steaks on the bone, cut 4cm thick*
olive oil for drizzling
salt and coarsely ground black pepper

Herbichurri sauce (chimichurri)
35g fresh flat-leaf parsley
70g fresh coriander
½ bulb fresh garlic, peeled and segmented
2 small red-eye chillies
1 tsp salt
1 tsp ground black pepper
¼ cup red wine vinegar
⅓ cup olive oil

Using a food processor or handheld blender, combine all the sauce ingredients and blitz until smooth.

Dry the steaks on both sides with paper towel until really dry. Drizzle with a little olive oil and pat a little salt and freshly cracked black pepper over the oil just before cooking.

To achieve a medium-rare result on a thick cut such as prime rib, high heat is necessary to seal in the juice. Grill the meat for 8 minutes on each side. For a medium finish, cook for 2 minutes longer on each side. For for well done, cook for about 5 minutes longer. Allow the meat to rest for at least 5 minutes before serving with the sauce.

Alternatively, try the stove-top-then-oven method. To turn out a perfect steak with a crispy crust encapsulating moist, tender meat, sear it first on the stove top and finish it in the oven. This is a great method of cooking, as long as you don't overcook the meat. (*In this case, the meat should be no less than 5cm thick.) Take the steak out of the refrigerator 1–2 hours before cooking. Preheat the oven to 240°C about 20 minutes before grilling.

Place a cast iron or oven-safe grill pan over a high heat on the stove top. Let it get hot enough that a flick of water instantly sizzles and evaporates. Paint a little more oil on both sides of the steaks, then place them on the smoking-hot grill pan, presentation-side down, and sear for 2 minutes without moving them. Turn the steaks with tongs and sear the other side in the same manner for another minute.

Transfer the grill pan to the middle rack of the hot oven and grill for 6–8 minutes. Check the temperature for 'doneness' (that thermometer you bought some time ago will finally come into use): rare is 50–60°C, medium is 60–70°C, and well done is 80°C (although some may prefer 75°C).

Remove the steaks from the grill pan once they are done to your satisfaction and place them on a plate to prevent further cooking from the oven heat. Leave them to rest for 5–10 minutes (tented in aluminium foil) to allow them to finish cooking and rise another five degrees. Be patient so that the juices settle back into the muscle fibres. It will be worth the wait. Serve with baked potatoes and the herbichurri sauce.

SERVES 4

Roll up for the longest list of ingredients rolled out in this book,
Roll up for one of the best tasting recipes you'll ever wrap your tongue around.
Roll up for some of the greatest spices and flavours you'll ever unfold,
Roll up for a dish like no other, because every ingredient is a drumroll.

Roll Up, Roll Up
DRUMROLL BEEF

---

2 Tbsp olive oil
2kg roll of beef
3 large onions, halved and thinly sliced
1 tsp crushed garlic
200g dried apricots, roughly chopped
2 stalks celery, sliced into 1cm lengths
8 prunes, halved and depipped
½ tsp dried rosemary
½ tsp dried thyme
2 tsp harissa spice
½ tsp ground cumin
½ tsp ground cinnamon
½ tsp paprika
½ tsp caraway seeds
½ tsp mustard seeds
½ tsp star anise
3 bay leaves
2 Tbsp honey
1½ cups red wine
1½ cups chicken stock
100g tomato paste
½ cup orange juice
½ tsp salt
½ tsp ground black pepper

Heat the oil in a large pot over a medium heat and brown the meat on all sides, then transfer to a cooking bag.

Preheat the oven to 180°C.

In the same pot in which the meat was browned, fry the onions, garlic, apricots, celery and prunes for about 10 minutes, stirring all the time over a medium heat. You may need to add a little more oil to the pot before frying the vegetables and fruit.

Once the onions are transparent, mix in the rosemary, thyme, harissa, cumin, cinnamon, paprika, caraway seeds, mustard seeds, star anise, bay leaves and honey, stirring all the time for 3 minutes. Add the red wine, chicken stock, tomato paste, orange juice, salt and pepper. Stir well and bring to the boil, then reduce the heat to a simmer and cook for another 3 minutes.

Pour the mixture over the meat in the cooking bag and seal it. Place the bag into a roasting dish and cook, uncovered, in the oven for 1 hour. Reduce the heat to 160°C, cover the roasting dish with aluminium foil (over the cooking bag) and continue cooking for another 2 hours.

Serve with your favourite vegetables.

SERVES 8

Why safari brisket? Purely because I was asked once to create a brisket for a deli with the flavours of Africa, rather than a typical New York-style brisket on rye, and so I share this with you ...

Safari BRISKET CROCKPOT

2–2.5kg fresh brisket
2 Tbsp cornflour
oil for frying
1 tsp Marmite dissolved in ½ cup boiling water
100g dried apricots
2 Tbsp smooth apricot jam
1 Tbsp Nando's peri-peri sauce (medium or hot)
½ cup chutney (mild or hot)
1 tsp grated fresh ginger
2 Tbsp tomato paste
4 cloves garlic
2 Tbsp onion soup powder
1 tsp curry powder
salt and pepper to taste

Rub the brisket in the cornflour. Heat a little oil in a pan and fry the meat until golden-brown. Make sure all outer surfaces are brown, because the crockpot won't brown the meat. Browning adds colour and helps to develop the flavour.

Place the rest of the ingredients either into the bowl of a food processor or into a jug (to use with a hand blender) and blend until well mixed. (This can be prepared a day or two before and stored in the fridge.)

Place the meat in a crockpot or slow cooker, cover with the blended mixture and cook on high for 1 hour, then turn down to low for another 8–10 hours. Alternatively, it can be cooked from the start on low for 11–12 hours. This is great served on a slice or two of s team-can mealie bread (page 44).

SERVES 6–8

South Africa's Liquor Act of 1927 prohibited black Africans from selling alcohol or entering licensed premises, while the Land Act, also of 1927, left the majority of the population without a source of income and thus had a dire economic effect on families. African women struggled to find employment and many returned to their former skills as beer-brewers (a customary role for women). Those who made and sold beer to migrant workers, who could not afford Western beers, were called Shebeen Queens. Shebeens were township bars and taverns, mostly where working-class men could unwind and escape the oppression of life in a segregated society. Despite their illegal status, these taverns played a unifying role in the community where cultural, political and social issues could be expressed. Post the 1994 elections, shebeens (many of which are now legal) became more sophisticated, catering for a younger, trendier generation of black and white patrons, and echo a jazzy feel with the music of greats such as Sipho Hotstix Mabuse, Mara Louw, Abigail Kubeka and Lucky Dube. South Africa is a country rich in culture, colour and food. To share a recipe is to share a meal!

During the week following a traditional Jewish wedding, festive get-togethers are held in honour of the couple, known as *Sheva Brachot* or seven blessings for the newlyweds. Family and friends gather to entertain the couple and themed dinners are arranged. My daughter and her friends decided to do a shebeen theme for newlywed friends and the potted bread, *dombolo*, *pap* and stews that rolled out of the kitchen certainly set the scene for a true infusion of heritage and culture. They had so much fun, and the use of minced beef enabled a free flow and the recipe to stretch well, especially in a situation where the number of guests was difficult to predict.

Easy Shebeen SHEVA BRACHOT CURRY

3 Tbsp oil
2 medium onions, chopped
1 tsp crushed garlic
1 Tbsp finely grated fresh ginger
2 fresh hot chillies, deseeded and chopped
1 tsp ground cumin
1 tsp ground turmeric
2.5kg beef mince
2 cups cold water
2 x 400g cans peeled and chopped tomatoes
2 Tbsp tomato paste
1 tsp sugar
salt to taste
¼ cup chopped fresh coriander
1 cup chutney

Heat the oil in a large pot, then brown the onions. Add the garlic, ginger and chillies and fry together for another 2 minutes. Add the cumin and turmeric and stir well. Add the mince, water, tomatoes, tomato paste and sugar and bring to the boil. Once boiling, break up the mince with a fork while stirring. Keep stirring until the meat is cooked through, otherwise it will go lumpy. Season with salt and give another good stir.

Finally, add the coriander and chutney, reduce the heat and leave to simmer, uncovered, over a low heat for approximately 30 minutes, stirring every 10 minutes or so to ensure it doesn't catch.

Switch the stove off and leave the pot on the plate for about 30 minutes to allow the meat to absorb the flavours. Reheat when ready to serve.

Serve with either *dombolo*, *pap*, roti, rice or in bread as a bunny chow.

SERVES 10–12

The base to this dish is a traditional bed of *umngqusho* (samp mealies and beans), which can be quite bland without seasoning. However, the spiced coating on this roll of beef certainly makes it a wonderful combination and the perfect pair. Samp is a South African dish of dried mealie kernels, which are stamped and crushed (losing their coating in the process), and is naturally gluten free.

SLOW-COOKED SPICY BEEF
with umngqusho

oil for frying
2kg deboned chuck or raisin rib
1 cup dried samp mielies, covered with water and soaked overnight
½ cup dried brown speckled beans, covered with water and soaked overnight
2 chicken stock cubes dissolved in 2 cups boiling water

Spice rub
1 Tbsp chilli flakes
2 Tbsp tomato paste
3 large cloves garlic, crushed (more if you like garlic)
¼ cup olive oil
½ tsp salt
1 Tbsp coarsely ground black pepper
1 tsp grated lemon zest
1 Tbsp lemon juice
2 Tbsp harissa paste
2 tsp soft brown sugar

Heat some oil in a large pan and fry the beef until golden-brown all over.

Meanwhile, drain the samp mielies and beans from the water in which they were soaking overnight and place in a crockpot or slow cooker.

Remove the meat from the pan and set aside. To the same pan, add the chicken stock and deglaze by scraping all the lovely bits of meat from the bottom of the pan.

Meanwhile, combine all the rub ingredients and spread over the meat, ensuring that it is well coated.

Pour the deglazed liquid from the pan over the samp and beans, then rest the meat on top. Cook on high for 2 hours, then reduce to low and continue cooking for another 4–6 hours. The meat should give off enough liquid while cooking, but if the samp and beans look as though they are drying out, add a little more water down the sides of the pot, but not directly over the meat.

SERVES 8

It was Shabbos *Nachamu* and the DL Link, a non-profit organisation that provides comprehensive, professional and expert support services to members affected by cancer, held 'The Pink Shabbos' – a Shabbos to raise awareness of those suffering with this dreaded disease.

Bakeries baked pink challahs. Shabbos kits were available that included pink serviettes, pink candles, pink flowers and so much more. In fact, the entire community was involved in the project. That week on the radio I gave suggestions for pink food, from fish in pink sauce to salads with pink salad dressing, pink desserts, strawberry ice cream and pink cookies. But a pink meat and pink vegetables? Was that pushing it? No, definitely not! And that is how tickled pink brisket came about. Pickled meat always turns pink when cooked. The beetroot was pink and turned the onions pink too.

TICKLED PINK BRISKET with roasted beetroot & onions

- 2.5kg pickled brisket or hump, washed well
- 4 bay leaves
- 1kg baby onions, peeled
- 3 Tbsp canola oil
- ½ cup brown sugar
- 1 tsp finely grated fresh ginger
- 1 tsp crushed garlic (optional)
- 1 heaped tsp raw or bottled horseradish
- 1 cup red wine
- ½ cup tomato purée
- 1 Tbsp crushed peppercorns
- 3 Tbsp smooth apricot jam
- 5 medium beetroot, boiled until cooked through, then peeled and quartered

Place the brisket or hump in a large pot and cover with water. Add the bay leaves and bring to the boil, then cook for 1 hour.

Preheat the oven to 160°C.

Meanwhile, in a large pan, fry the onions in the oil until golden-brown. Add the sugar, ginger, garlic (if using), horseradish and wine and leave to simmer for 5 minutes, allowing the sauce to reduce just a little. Mix in the tomato purée, peppercorns and jam until well incorporated.

Place the meat in a cooking bag and pour in the sauce. Slice the beetroot into quarters, then gently place them on either side of the meat in the cooking bag. Seal the bag with a wire tie and roast for 4–5 hours.

Serve with a salad of your choice.

SERVES 10

One of my most popular Shabbos lunches ever, which has subsequently become a regular, was this meat dish. The beef cooks all night in a crockpot and is served, piled high, on a thick slice of challah. The glazed raisin rib falls apart and is delicious on the challah, which acts as an absorbent mop for all the lovely juices. Sometimes I add potatoes to the crockpot and at other times I make a potato salad to serve with it. Either way, it's a winner every time.

All-Night SHREDDED BEEF

- 2 cups barbecue sauce (your favourite brand) or homemade monkey gland sauce (page 184)
- 2 Tbsp wholegrain mustard
- 3 Tbsp brown onion soup powder
- 2 cups cola
- 3 Tbsp tomato paste
- 3kg raisin rib (chuck off the bone)
- 12 large potatoes (optional)

Combine the barbecue or monkey gland sauce, mustard, soup powder, cola and tomato paste until well mixed.

Place the raisin rib in a crockpot and arrange the potatoes (if using) around the meat. Cover all with the sauce mixture. This can cook in the crockpot on the low setting from sunset until lunchtime the following day. As it is a very forgiving cut of meat, it enjoys the slow cook. However, if you're a little more rushed, it may be cooked on high for 4 hours during the day, then turned down to low for another 6–8 hours.

Another option is to roast the meat in the oven overnight at 110°C, but if you're including potatoes, more liquid (about 2 cups) will be needed, as it is a dryer heat than crockpot cooking. Also ensure that the roasting dish isn't too large for the meat, otherwise the sauce will evaporate and cook out too quickly.

SERVES 12

LAMB

Lamb chops are always a favourite for supper, although the classic combination of salt and pepper and barbecue spice can sometimes become a bit repetitive. These delicious pastes are the perfect flavour updates.

THE BIG FIVE

1. Mix 2 tablespoons of harissa paste, 2 teaspoons of olive oil and 1 tablespoon of chopped fresh mint. Rub into lamb chops. Sear in a frying pan.
2. Rub lamb chops with a mixture of 2 tablespoons of olive oil, half a teaspoon of ground cinnamon, 1 crushed garlic clove, 1 teaspoon of ground cumin and the juice of 1 lemon. Leave to marinate for as long as you can (up to 3 hours) and sear in a frying pan. Sprinkle lightly with dukkah spice just before serving.
3. Brush lamb chops with a mixture of 2 tablespoons of smooth apricot jam, 1 tablespoon of sesame oil, 1 teaspoon of fresh minced ginger and a dash of soy sauce, then grill.
4. Grill or sear lamb chops sliced very thinly (0.5cm), then drizzle with tahini sauce made with 3 tablespoons of tahini paste, 2 teaspoons of chopped fresh parsley, 1 crushed garlic clove and 1 tablespoon of freshly squeezed lemon juice. Serve on a bed of rocket, watercress and lettuce.
5. Combine 1 tablespoon of chopped fresh rosemary with 2 tablespoons of olive oil and 2 tablespoons of balsamic vinegar. Rub into lamb chops and grill.

EACH MAKES ENOUGH PASTE FOR 4–6 LAMB CHOPS

I was taught to prepare lamb biryani by rubbing the ingredients listed below over the lamb the night before. This dish has such a wonderful combination of flavours and the beauty of it is that most of us have these ingredients in our cupboards, which makes it even easier to enjoy. Of course there is a plethora of biryani variations, with different combinations of meat and vegetables, and the spice mixtures varying by region. This is my version.

LAMB BIRYANI

1.5kg cubed lamb, on the bone
cooking oil for frying
1 large onion, finely chopped
1 tsp ground cumin
1 tsp ground turmeric
1 tsp garam masala
3 cardamom pods, crushed to release seeds
1 stick cinnamon or 1 tsp ground cinnamon
2 tsp grated fresh ginger
salt and pepper to taste
3 cloves garlic, crushed
½ cup finely chopped dried apricots
1 cup basmati rice*
1 cup boiling water
1 cube vegetable stock dissolved in 1 cup boiling water
1 x 410g can chopped tomatoes (preferably Indian-style chopped tomatoes)
1 tsp sugar
2 large potatoes, peeled and cubed
fresh mint and coriander for serving

Rub

1 heaped tsp minced garlic
1 tsp chilli flakes
1 Tbsp grated fresh ginger
2 tsp sweet paprika
1 tsp coarsely ground black pepper

Combine all the rub ingredients, then massage into the meat and leave overnight, or for at least 6 hours, in the refrigerator.

Fry the lamb in a heavy-based pot (with a lid) in a little oil until golden-brown. Remove from the pot and set aside. (Don't wash the pot – you need all the lovely caramelised bits at the bottom to add flavour to the vegetables.)

To the same pot, add a little more oil and fry the onion until soft (about 4 minutes). Stir in the cumin, turmeric, garam masala, cardamom, cinnamon, ginger, salt and pepper, then fry for 2 minutes to bring out all the flavours. Add the garlic and apricots and cook for a further 2 minutes.

Return the meat to the pot. Add the prepared rice (see below) and stir well to ensure that all the grains are coated with the onion mixture. Add the boiling water, vegetable stock, tomatoes, sugar and potatoes. If the lid of the pot doesn't fit tightly enough, make a thick paste of flour and water to run around the seal of the pot lid and press down onto the pot. Alternatively, use a muslin cloth between the lid and the pot. Biryani enjoys steam cooking. (In fact, some of my best biryanis have been those transferred to a crockpot after the potatoes were added.)

When the vegetables and meat are done to desired tenderness (approximately 1 hour), remove from the heat and serve with chopped fresh mint and coriander.

*Rinse the rice with cold water until the water is no longer cloudy (3 or 4 times), then leave to sit covered in boiling water with 2 bay leaves for about 30 minutes until ready to use. Discard any excess water and the bay leaves before using.

SERVES 4–6

It's very difficult not to be greedy with this tomato *bredie*. It's one of those dishes that are great in a potjie over coals or a heavy-based pot on your kitchen stove. This is a traditional South African meal, and is good winter fare. *Bredie* is an old Cape name for a dish of meat stewed with delicious herbs and spices so that the flavours really intermingle. The gravy is rich, thick and full-bodied, and nobody praised *bredies* better than poet-physician C. Louis Leipoldt in his book *Cape Cookery*: '… the free, almost heroic, use of spices and aromatic flavouring … a combination of meat and vegetables so intimately stewed that the flesh is thoroughly impregnated with the vegetable flavour while the vegetables have benefited from the meat fluids. Neither dominates but both combine to make a delectable whole that is a triumph of cooperative achievement.'

The flavour improves if left a day or two before eating. We love this dish with sides of sweet potatoes and crunchy green beans.

TOMATO BREDIE

2kg neck of lamb or stewing lamb
½ cup cake flour mixed with 2 Tbsp onion soup powder
sunflower oil for frying
½ cup cold water
1 tsp crushed fresh garlic
1 stick cinnamon
4 whole cloves
1 tsp paprika
1 x 410g can chopped and peeled tomatoes
1 x 410g can Indian-style tomatoes (or another can chopped tomatoes)
4 cardamom pods
2 Tbsp tomato paste
1 tsp sugar
2 beef stock cubes dissolved in 1½ cups boiling water
2 Tbsp tomato jam (or apricot if tomato unavailable)
juice of 1 freshly squeezed orange
1 tsp grated orange rind
1 glug sherry or Shabbos wine (optional)
1 heaped tsp brown sugar
1 tsp dried or a few sprigs fresh thyme

Roll the lamb in the flour and onion soup mixture.

In a large, heavy-based pot, brown the lamb in a little oil. Fry small batches at a time. Remove from the pot and set aside.

In the same pot, pour in the water followed by the rest of the ingredients and keep stirring to combine and prevent them from sticking to the bottom of the pot. Bring to the boil, then return the lamb to the pot. Give it a good stir and make sure the meat is covered by the sauce. Allow the meat to simmer, covered, for about 30 minutes over a low heat. It should make its own liquid, but if the sauce becomes too thick, add a little more water. It's better to have extra water that cooks out when the lid is removed than too little and the food burns. Continue to simmer until the meat is soft, stirring every now and then to prevent any burning.

Serve on a bed of sweet potato mash with green beans.

SERVES 6–8

As the Voortrekkers didn't have the space to transport many pots on their journeys into the interior during the Great Trek, a one-pot meal known as *potjiekos* (pronounced poy-key-cos and meaning 'small pot food' in Afrikaans) was born out of necessity to simplify cooking. A three-legged cast iron pot is filled with meat, starch and vegetables, seasoned with spices and covered with a lid. Hot coals are then scraped underneath the pot to create an all-round moist heat, capable of tenderising the toughest of meat. Only if you suspect that there isn't enough liquid are you allowed to pour in a little down the sides of the pot, never in the middle! A typical *potjiekos* takes 2½ to 3 hours to cook.

What makes *potjiekos* so great and versatile is that there is no one, particular recipe. You can't be told 'That's not a potjie' as that would be *loshen hora* (bad tongue wagging), so the play on words with the title of this *potjie* is therefore quite simple. Not only do I use lamb shanks (also called shin) in the recipe, but you dare not speak badly of it either. There is one rule that differentiates this dish from a stew ... NEVER STIR it once you've layered the ingredients (meat, vegetables and finally potato or rice to seal the deal) and the lid is on. Whether it's a selection of sausages, a variety of vegetables or a mixture of different meats, *gaan mal* (go crazy) experimenting and prepare yourself for the next *potjiekos* competition.

No Loshin POTJIEKOS

---

2 Tbsp sunflower oil
1.5kg meaty lamb shanks, sliced 5cm thick
¼ cup cake flour or gluten-free flour
1kg baby onions
500g baby carrots
3 leeks, roughly chopped
2 stalks celery, chopped
1 tsp crushed fresh garlic
1 tsp salt
1 cup red wine
2 cups beef stock (2 heaped Tbsp beef stock powder dissolved in 2 cups boiling water)
3 Tbsp smooth apricot jam
100g dried apricots, finely chopped
1 x 410g can chopped Indian-style tomatoes or 1 x 410g chopped tomatoes with 1 Tbsp curry powder stirred in
2 heaped Tbsp tomato paste
5 sprigs fresh thyme
4 sprigs fresh rosemary
1 tsp crushed black pepper
1kg baby potatoes, halved

In a large cast iron pot (it's up to you whether to use a flat-bottomed pot as I do on the stove top or a three-legged *potjie* over coals), heat the sunflower oil.

Dust the shanks with the flour, then fry in the oil for about 2 minutes per side until golden-brown. Add a layer of onions, carrots, leeks, celery and garlic. Sprinkle a little salt between each layer. Pour in the wine and bring to the boil, allowing it to boil for 5 minutes. Add the stock, apricot jam, dried apricots, tomatoes, tomato paste, thyme, rosemary and pepper. Finally, cover with the baby potatoes.

Place the lid on the pot and leave the stew to cook slowly over medium heat or open coals, or over a low heat on the stove top, until beautifully tender.

SERVES 6–8

So what's the DNA of a Durban curry, this national treasure of a dish, known and loved around South Africa and beyond?

Even acknowledged exponents on the art of curry are at odds on the subject. 'But what are its distinguishing, vital statistics?' asks Erica Platter, author of the Gourmand award-winning book *Durban Curry*. 'It could be the bold use of spices and the majestic red colour that makes Durban curry so unique.' But for my penny's worth, very ripe red tomatoes must be included to make it red and real chillies to make it hot! And surely it's all about the mystery of family traditions?

It's always preferable to prepare this dish the day before you're going to serve it, as it always tastes better on the second day.

DURBAN CURRY

2 Tbsp oil
1.5kg stewing lamb, on the bone
4 onions, chopped
1 tsp fennel seeds
1 Tbsp finely grated fresh ginger
3 cloves garlic, crushed
1 or 2 chillies, deseeded and chopped (depends how hot you like it!)
2 bay leaves
18 fresh curry leaves or 1 Tbsp dried curry leaves
2 sticks cinnamon
3 Tbsp Durban masala or red curry powder
2 tsp garam masala
1 tsp ground cumin
4 cardamom pods
1 tsp ground turmeric
3 ripe red tomatoes, peeled, seeded and chopped
2 cups water
4 large potatoes, cubed
fresh coriander for serving

Heat the oil in a large pot and fry the meat until golden-brown. Remove the meat from the pot and set aside.

In the same pot, fry the onions until transparent, then add the fennel, ginger, garlic, chillies, bay leaves, curry leaves, cinnamon, Durban masala, garam masala, cumin, cardamom and turmeric, and fry for another minute. Finally, add the tomatoes and give it a good stir.

Add the water and mix well. Return the lamb to the pot, bring to the boil and allow to simmer for 45 minutes before adding the potatoes. Continue to simmer for another 30 minutes or until the potatoes are soft and the meat is tender. Stir every now and then to ensure that it is not sticking to the bottom of the pot.

Sprinkle fresh coriander over the curry just before serving with rice.

SERVES 6–8

CHICKEN

One of the perks of hosting the Cookery Corner on Chai FM is that I meet and interview such interesting people; authors, cooks and real foodies. One such was Hope Malau, author of *Johanne 14*. In this book he tells a story that reminds me of *gribenes* (fried chicken skin) and I just have to share it. Hope says: 'Sold at township butcheries, chicken skins are super cheap, perfect for when a mother has to provide a heart-warming meal with the little she has.'

Many of the younger generation would shudder at such a recipe, but it is unprocessed and chemical free, and it's what kept our grandparents, their parents, and theirs before them, warm and healthy in winter.

On a recent visit to New York, I was taken aback to see some of the top bars and restaurants there serving crispy fried battered chicken skins with a dipping sauce on the side. Not to mention chicken feet, which have become very trendy, cooked almost as they are in South Africa, bar a few twists, then spiced, fried or braaied until crispy and served with a house sauce. In South Africa chicken feet are called 'runaways', and, as a friend once said, 'The greatest cure for a hangover is peri-peri-spiced runaways.'

So it's back to basics with my mother's recipe for *schmaltz* (chicken fat), made from chicken skin. The rendered crispy skin is absolutely delicious crumbled over a salad or used in a potato pudding. Don't forget to ask your butcher for chicken skins. With so many people using only skinless chicken portions, the skin has to go somewhere!

MAMMA, GIMME SOME SKIN AND SCHMALTZ

500g chicken skins, well washed
1 large onion, quartered
1 large carrot, sliced into 2–3cm rounds
2 cups boiling water
250g Holsum solid vegetable fat

Add the skins, onion and carrot to a saucepan and cover with the water. Cook, with the lid loosely on top, until the water has evaporated and the fat begins to crackle. Once the skins start to fry, add the vegetable fat and continue frying over a low heat, uncovered, until the skins start to crisp. Take care not to let them burn, as the *schmaltz* will taste bitter.

Strain through a muslin cloth or a fine strainer, and remove the carrot and onion bits but keep them for your next pot of chicken soup. Refrigerate the liquid gold. (There's enough deliciousness in that little saucepan to allow even your cardiologist to turn a blind eye!)

What should remain in the muslin cloth are crispy, dark golden *gribenes*. If you like, you can crisp them up further in the oven at 140°C.

MAKES 1 CUP OF *SCHMALTZ*

These hot and spicy wings are a must as a starter straight off the braai or as a main meal with a soothing dipping sauce – this would be a good time to challenge yourself in the hot (spicy) sauce race. The heat of most sauces is rated from one to ten; see how high you can climb. Don't forget that the wings must be marinated overnight.

HOT WINGS over Africa

3 fresh red chillies, finely chopped
1 cup tomato ketchup or sauce
⅓ cup freshly squeezed lemon juice
2 tsp crushed fresh garlic
2 tsp dried coriander
½ cup honey or soft brown sugar
½ cup of your favourite peri-peri sauce (I prefer Nando's hot peri-peri sauce)
30 chicken wings
salt and pepper to taste

Soothing dip

1 English cucumber, grated
1 cup mayonnaise
salt and pepper to taste

In a bowl, combine the chillies, tomato ketchup or sauce, lemon juice, garlic, coriander, honey or brown sugar and peri-peri sauce, and mix well. Sprinkle the wings with salt and pepper and place them into a large Ziploc bag. Cover with the sauce mixture, seal the bag and marinate overnight.

The following day, remove the wings from the bag and either braai them or roast them until dark and crispy for about 1 hour, uncovered, in an oven preheated to 180°C.

If there is any sauce remaining in the bag, bring it to the boil in a small saucepan, then drizzle over the chicken before serving. This sauce MUST be boiled as it previously had raw chicken marinating in it.

For the dip, remove any excess liquid by pressing the cucumber through a strainer with the back of a spoon. Add the mayonnaise and salt and pepper, then stir well.

Arrange the wings around a bowl of the dip and serve.

SERVES 10–12

It was my nephew's destination wedding in Jamaica. Somehow, I could have been in my hometown of Durban. Perhaps it was the colonial-style homes and the bougainvillea draped everywhere, cascading down from the highest of pillars, or the palm tree-lined roads that led to calm beaches, where water gently rolled up and down the white sand that surrounded the cabanas of our resort. If the aroma of Blue Mountain coffee and coconut rum cocktails was a hint of what was to come, it promised to be a culinary experience like no other. Jamaica is famous for its jerk chicken and, although not traditionally South African, it has become so popular here that I think we make it as often as the Jamaicans do.

Joburg-Style JERK CHICKEN

1 spatchcocked chicken
1 lime

Marinade
1 cup chopped spring onions
8 cloves garlic
5cm piece fresh ginger, roughly chopped
1 Scotch bonnet pepper, intense hot orange or red in colour
2 Tbsp dried thyme
2 Tbsp vegetable oil
2 Tbsp apple cider vinegar
2 Tbsp brown sugar
2 tsp ground allspice
juice of 2 oranges
2 tsp grated nutmeg

Place all the marinade ingredients into the bowl of a food processor and blend until smooth. Spread this mixture over the chicken and leave it to marinate overnight.

If you are having a braai, make sure that the coals have been burning for an hour or so before you barbecue the chicken. Authentic jerked meats are not exactly grilled as we think of grilling, but sort of smoke-grilled. For a more authentic jerk experience, add some wood chips to the barbecue, then cook the chicken over slow, indirect heat for 1–1½ hours. Just before serving, squeeze the juice of a lime over the chicken.

To cook in the oven, preheat to 180°C. Place the chicken in a roasting dish, uncovered, with the lime cut in half, then roast for 1 hour. Reduce the heat to 160°C and roast for a further 30 minutes.

Serve with rice.

SERVES 6

My cousin Kate was out here from the UK and remembered that she wanted to make her one-pot comfort chicken for us for dinner one night. Caring is sharing, cousin, so into the kitchen we went where we created her chicken pot 'my way'. It certainly isn't a bowl of soup, although it would be acceptable and possibly easier to eat with a spoon. The beauty of this dish is that you can add any vegetable that takes your fancy. Whether it's cubed butternut, courgettes, broccoli, green beans or cauliflower, it will add to a meal that is power-packed with everything that is good for you.

Kneidlach (dumplings) are traditionally made with matzah meal, but for the purposes of this dish, because the balls are so small, self-raising flour or cornmeal (not cornflour) is suitable. They can be prepared a day ahead, and thereafter refrigerated (covered).

RUSTIC CHICKEN COMFORT POT with kneidlach

1 whole chicken, cut into portions
2 Tbsp cooking oil
2 onions, diced
3 stalks celery, finely sliced on the diagonal
3 large carrots, grated
2 leeks, finely chopped
250g mushrooms, sliced
2 cups frozen peas
1 cup uncooked brown rice
2 large potatoes, cubed
optional vegetables (your choice)
3 litres water (possibly a little more)
3 bay leaves
¼ cup chicken stock powder
salt and pepper to taste

***Kneidlach* (dumplings)**
2 extra-large eggs
½ cup water
2 Tbsp vegetable oil
1 tsp salt
a pinch white pepper
¾ cup matzah meal, or slightly more if using self-raising flour or cornmeal

In a large soup pot, fry the chicken portions with their skin in the oil until golden-brown. Remove from the pot and set aside to cool. Once cool, debone and cut into smaller pieces.

While the chicken is cooling, add the onions, celery, carrots, leeks and mushrooms to the same pot, then fry until softened. Add the peas, rice, potatoes, any other vegetables (if using), water and bay leaves, and bring to the boil. Add the raw *kneidlach* (dumplings) (see below). Once the dumplings are soft, return the cooled chicken pieces to the pot, along with the chicken stock powder. Mix carefully until warmed through. I prefer to add the stock powder at the end, because the vegetables take longer to cook if the liquid thickens too soon from the powder. Finally, season with salt and pepper.

To make the *kneidlach* , whisk the eggs in a bowl until smooth, then whisk in the water, oil, salt and pepper. Add the matzah meal or flour or cornmeal, a little at a time, and mix until the ingredients are well combined to form a dough. If not preparing them the day before, cover and refrigerate for 1 hour.

Flour a working surface. Roll the dough into ropes of about 1cm in diameter and then cut them into 2cm pieces, just as you would gnocchi. Drop them into the simmering liquid, as per the instructions above. However, if you're going to boil them separately, bring a pot of salted water to the boil and drop them in. Cover and boil for 30 minutes. When steam begins to escape from the pot, reduce the heat a little so that it's still boiling, but less vigorously.

Serve the dumplings in the chicken stew, if they aren't already in it.

SERVES 6–8

Sriracha is a wonderful, reddish orange-coloured sauce, available from most supermarkets; one of those that says, 'Try me, you won't be sorry.' Nor will you be disappointed after tasting the combination of flavours in this recipe. South Africans love spicy food, so this Thai hot sauce named after the city in which it was first made, Sri Racha, on the coast of Thailand, is the perfect condiment with just about everything. In fact, a friend of my son's asked for it with his omelette, and told me that his girlfriend loves it over a bowl of plain rice.

SRIRACHA AND HONEY CHICKEN

3 cloves garlic
⅓ cup honey
⅓ cup sriracha chilli sauce
2 Tbsp soy sauce
2 Tbsp rice vinegar or apple cider vinegar
3 Tbsp sesame oil
1 chicken braai pack, with 10 portions
oil for frying
fresh coriander and sesame seeds for garnishing

Preheat the oven to 180°C.

Combine the garlic, honey, sriracha sauce, soy sauce, rice vinegar or apple cider vinegar and sesame oil.

Fry the chicken portions in oil (or you could braai them if you like), then transfer them to an ovenproof dish, pour over the sauce and bake for 45 minutes, until cooked through. Sprinkle with fresh coriander and sesame seeds.

Serve with bowls of rice.

SERVES 6

I have to admit, I have gone coconut crazy! Coconut milk, coconut cream, coconut oil and coconut flour. This dish has become one of my favourites on a cold winter's night.

CHICKEN AND COCONUT BOWLS
with coriander dombolo (dumplings)

1 Tbsp sesame oil, plus extra
1 Tbsp canola oil
500g chicken thighs or breasts, cut schuwarma style (1 x 2cm)
1 onion, cut into 8 wedges and leaves separated
2 leeks, chopped into 2cm pieces
1 heaped Tbsp Thai green curry paste
1 heaped tsp grated ginger
½ tsp crushed fresh garlic
1 tsp ground turmeric
1 fresh green chilli, finely chopped
1 litre good quality chicken stock
2 sticks lemon grass, bruised (roll over with a rolling pin)
1 tsp salt
1 x 410ml can coconut milk
1 green pepper, deseeded and sliced
1 small red pepper, deseeded and sliced
1 cup frozen corn, defrosted
100g pak choy or baby spinach, chopped
juice of 1 lime
fresh peas and baby corn for garnishing

Coriander *dombolo*
2 cups cake flour
¼ tsp salt
2 Tbsp baking powder
2 heaped Tbsp non-dairy margarine (e.g. Holsum)
1 cup coconut or soya milk
1 egg
a handful fresh coriander, chopped

To make the *dombolo* (dumplings or *kneidlach*), combine the flour, salt and baking powder. Add the margarine and mix with the tips of your fingers until it resembles fine crumbs. Add the milk and egg and stir to form a soft dough. Add the coriander and mix into the dough. Refrigerate for 30–40 minutes.

Meanwhile, heat the sesame and canola oils in a deep frying pan. Add the chicken pieces and fry until lightly caramelised. Remove the chicken and set aside. To the same pan, add a little more sesame oil, then fry the onion and leeks for 1–2 minutes (don't cook them too long, as they shouldn't be too soft). Add the curry paste, ginger, garlic, turmeric and chilli and mix until well combined. Add the chicken stock and lemon grass and bring to the boil. Reduce the heat and leave to simmer for 30 minutes with the lid lying loosely on top.

Bring a pot of water with the salt to the boil. Drop the dumpling dough by the teaspoonful into the water. (A teaspoonful may seem rather small, but bite-size dumplings are nicer.) Boil for 10 minutes, then switch off the heat and leave in the water with the pot covered.

Return to the frying pan and add the coconut milk, green and red peppers, corn, pak choy and chicken pieces. Bring to the boil again, then reduce the heat and stir in the lime juice. Remove the dumplings from their pot with a slotted spoon and add to the chicken dish.

Garnish with fresh peas and baby corn. Serve in bowls.

SERVES 8–10

HERE COMES THE BRAAI'D

My favourite method of cooking is braaiing. There's a ridiculous notion among South Africans that women cannot braai, which leads me to wonder just why women don't braai more often.

My husband works with meat all day – smoking, cooking, cutting – so the last thing he feels like is doing that all over again when he gets home. My love of flame-licked meat has conquered any fear I might once have had of cooking over an open fire. Whether I'm braaiing lamb shanks and then slow roasting them afterwards, barbecuing a brisket or sizzling a steak, the flare of the flame just does it for me! And with the power outages we often experience in South Africa, a braai is the answer; whether it's gas or coal depends on time, weather and personal preference. Most of my beef roasts are started off on a braai and transferred to my oven; chicken always tastes better on the braai; and, as for lamb, that flame just takes it to a whole new level.

On the subject of flames, let's chat about *shisa nyama*, an isiZulu word literally meaning 'burn meat'; not burnt meat, but rather flame-licked braai meat. It's used to describe a popular 'buy-and-braai' style of venue found across South Africa. This is also available 'kosher' in Johannesburg at Nussbaums Kosher Butcher and Prime Grill in Glenhazel, where your favourite steak or Shabbos cut can be grilled and either taken home for the family to enjoy or eaten there. At a *shisa nyama*, you choose your own meat from the butchery and then have it barbecued to your exact taste. Many a township *shisa nyama* will create a weekend party atmosphere with DJs and bars, while others cater to the urban workforce, looking for quick and easy street-side food on their lunch break.

South Africa just wouldn't be the same without the ever-so-popular braai. Enjoyed by all cultures, braaiing is a social event focused around quality meat and good food, and guests normally dine outside. Many households braai at least once a week. Every genuine meat lover should experience a braai at least once, and it's worth travelling to South Africa just to attend one. In fact, there is even a day known unofficially as National Braai Day, celebrated annually on the official public holiday of Heritage Day on 24 September.

You don't need too many spices, as the chimichurri does it all.

RIB EYE STEAKS IN ROOSTERKOEK
with red chimichurri salsa

olive oil
8 x 200g rib eye steaks
salt and pepper to taste
8 *roosterkoek* (page 42)
red chimichurri salsa (page 188)

Start by preparing your barbecue or braai.

Rub olive oil over the steaks, then sprinkle them with salt and pepper. Braai them over hot coals according to your preferred method of braaiing (whether an open fire or a kettle braai).

Meanwhile, make the *roosterkoek*. While the dough is rising you can make the red chimichurri salsa. It's as simple as that…

Serve the steaks on the *roosterkoek* with the salsa. And don't forget the ice-cold beers!

SERVES 8

STAINLESS ROSTFREI INOX

I know that the thought of monkey gland sauce is making you say squeamishly, 'Hey, we're not Andrew Zimmern, we don't eat such bizarre things!' In fact, there is no 'monkey' or 'gland' in the sauce, and where the name comes from remains a mystery. However, it's delicious and addictive, especially with a grilled steak. Once you've tried South Africa's favourite barbecue sauce, you'll never want another one. It turns these simple steakhouse ribs into a mouthwatering experience!

This recipe can also be prepared with sliced 'Chinese-style' top rib.

MONKEY GLAND BRAAI RIBS

3 racks smoked or fresh steakhouse ribs, ± 12cm in length
1 x monkey gland sauce (page 184)

Preheat the oven to 180°C.

Either brown the ribs on a braai over flames or fry them in a wok or large frying pan, meaty-side down first, then on the remaining sides until evenly tanned.

Transfer to a roasting dish*, meaty-side up (facing you). Pour over the sauce, ensuring that the ribs are generously coated. Roast for 45–60 minutes, uncovered, then reduce the heat to 170°C and continue to roast, covered, for another hour until tender. Uncover and check that they are well glazed. If too dry, add a little more sauce and continue to cook covered. (So you're cooking these for almost 2 hours in total from initial browning to time in the oven.) If the sauce seems too runny, leave the dish open and continue to roast until it thickens into a lovely glaze.

*I have also roasted the ribs in a transparent cooking bag with great success, not only because they turn a lovely dark colour, but because they stay moist as well. If they look as though they're becoming too dark, just cover the cooking bag in the roasting dish with aluminium foil.

SERVES 4–6

Side bolo is the only cut to use for this recipe. Cut the meat in half lengthwise, butterflying it so that you can remove the white sinew in the middle.

How lucky I was that my brother had trimmed his bay leaf tree. My nieces sat for 2 hours stripping leaves off branches, which we threaded onto the skewers alternating with the meat. Thereafter, we used the thin branches as threading sticks instead of regular wooden skewers. Simply marinated and grilled, these sosaties need very little to accompany them. If you don't have bay leaf branch stems to thread through the meat, pre-soaked wooden skewers will do.

MOZAMBICAN MARINATED BEEFSTICKS

1–1.5kg side bolo, halved horizontally through the middle, sinew removed and cut into 3cm cubes
1 large red pepper, deseeded and cut into 3x3cm cubes
1 large onion, cut into chunks
wooden skewers, soaked in warm water for 30 minutes

Marinade

1 cup monkey gland sauce (page 184 or readymade)
¼ cup soy sauce
a handful fresh coriander, finely chopped
½ cup brown sugar
6 large cloves garlic, crushed
2 hot chillies, finely chopped
3 bay leaves, plus extra for grilling
½ tsp freshly ground black pepper
3 Tbsp red wine vinegar

To prepare the marinade, combine the ingredients. Put the meat cubes in a shallow, non-reactive bowl and pour the marinade over them. Turn the meat to coat thoroughly on all sides and allow to marinate overnight in the refrigerator.

When ready to cook or braai the sosaties, thread the cubes of meat, alternating with red peppers and onion chunks, onto the skewers. Grill over a medium heat until golden-brown and cooked to your desired doneness.

SERVES 6

SOSATIES – THE SOCIABLE STICK

My nephew and his wife, who live in the US, came to South Africa for their honeymoon. And, typically for us, we had our entire extended family over to meet the new *kallah* (wife). So Sunday was braai night and it was going to be a variety of meats on sticks – kebabs, or sosaties to us. Lamb, beef, chicken, boerewors and vegetables; a combination of wonderful meats and African spices and herbs with dipping sauces to accompany them.

What I love about sosaties is their versatility and unpretentious informality. The word 'sosatie' is of Cape Malay origin, via Afrikaans, and it is used to describe most types of skewered meat. Although traditionally it was meant for marinated cubed meat such as lamb, which is thereafter braaied (barbecued), now you can use beef, chicken, fish, dried apricots, red onions, mixed peppers and various other vegetables. Whether you call them kebabs or sosaties, and whatever ingredients you use, the one rule is that these bite-size treats threaded onto skewers should look appealing and taste delicious. They cook quickly and are perfect straight off the braai as a snack, or as a main course with all the trimmings.

'Boerewors' literally means 'farmers sausage' in Afrikaans. A savoury sausage developed by farmers some 200 years ago, it is spiced predominantly with coriander, nutmeg, salt and pepper. *Pap* is made from mealie meal (maize meal) in South Africa. Once this meal is mixed with water and boiled until firm (almost like polenta), it starts to take on its characteristic *pap* texture. *Pap* and *wors* served with a savoury tomato sauce is South African food at its most traditional!

This recipe is a simple twist on the traditional version, its novelty being that the boerewors and *mieliepap* are threaded onto a stick, glazed and then braaied. The only problem with this finger-friendly way of serving the dish is that the *braaier* (griller) and his friends stand around the fire chatting, drinking beers and eating the kebabs before they even reach the table! So you may as well give them the dipping sauce upfront! And do remember that you can prepare the sauce in advance and reheat it.

GLAZED PAP AND WORS KEBABS with tomato & onion dipping sauce

1kg boerewors
12 wooden kebab sticks

Mieliepap balls
1½ cups mealie meal (finely ground maize meal)
1 x 420g can cream-style sweetcorn

Glaze
1 cup sweet chilli sauce
½ cup mild or hot chutney, or
2 Tbsp mild tomato salsa mixed with
1 Tbsp apricot jam

Dipping sauce
1 x 400g can tomato and onion mix
1 Tbsp apricot jam
1 Tbsp cornflour dissolved in ½ cup cold water

To make the *mieliepap* balls, use a large pot to cook the mealie meal as per the instructions on the packet. The meal must be firm enough to roll into balls when cool. Once all the meal is cooked, add the sweetcorn and mix well. Reduce the heat to low and allow to simmer, covered, for 15–20 minutes. Once cooked, transfer to a bowl and leave to cool.

While the *mieliepap* is cooking, soak the sticks in water (this prevents them from burning), and cook the boerewors (covered in paper towel) in a microwave oven on high for 8–10 minutes, or fry it over a low heat on the stove top. Leave it to cool, then cut into 4cm pieces. (The boerewors must be cooked before it's cut so that it doesn't fall apart when threaded onto the sticks.)

When the *mieliepap* mixture has cooled, roll spoonfuls into small balls (smaller than golf balls). Thread pieces of boerewors, alternating with *mieliepap* balls, onto the soaked sticks (press the balls firmly around the sticks), leaving approximately 4cm at the bottom for holding the sticks.

Mix the glaze ingredients together, then paint the kebabs with it. Braai or fry the kebabs on a flat skillet until golden-brown. Because they are already cooked, all you need to do is brown them, heat through and serve with the dipping sauce.

For the dipping sauce, combine the ingredients in a pot and bring to the boil. Lower the heat and simmer for 1–2 minutes, stirring continuously.

SERVES 6

You will need extra-thin skewers, to avoid breaking the liver when threading it. Thread aromatic leaves between the livers.

Quick and Easy PERI-PERI LIVER SOSATIES

500g ready-grilled chicken livers
6–8 extra-thin sosatie sticks

Peri-peri sauce
2 large onions, chopped
1 heaped tsp crushed garlic
3 Tbsp oil
1 cup red wine
1 Tbsp brown sugar
100g tomato paste
3 Tbsp hot chilli sauce (e.g. Nando's hot)
3 Tbsp sweet chilli sauce
1 beef stock cube dissolved in 1 cup boiling water
1 chicken stock cube dissolved in 1 cup boiling water

Wash the chicken livers well to remove any burnt edges, and separate the two halves to extract the middle vein.

In a large frying pan, fry the onions and garlic in the oil until lightly browned. Add the red wine, brown sugar and tomato paste, and bring to the boil. Reduce the heat and leave to simmer for about 5 minutes.

Add both the chilli sauces and livers to the pan, followed by the beef and chicken stocks, stirring lightly so as not to break the livers. Reduce the heat to low and simmer for 20 minutes, covered. (Although already grilled, the livers must be cooked again to absorb flavour and to comply with Kashrut law.) Switch off the heat and allow the livers to cool before threading them onto the sticks. (Retain the leftover peri-peri sauce.)

Just before serving, baste the sosaties with the leftover peri-peri sauce and reheat in a preheated oven at 200°C, or reheat the sauce as a dipping sauce and serve the sosaties with rice, polenta, mealie meal or Portuguese rolls.

SERVES 3–4

While watching pole vaulters on TV, I decided to make sosaties with a difference. I bent a dowel stick gently around a kettle braai. My guests applauded my new culinary heights! The result? A 1m-long sosatie that could be shared by all.

POLE VAULT SAUSAGE SOSATIES

500g Russian sausages
500g Vienna sausages
500g sliced polony
2 x dowel sticks, each 1m x 3mm
1 red pepper, sliced into 2cm squares
1 green pepper, sliced into 2cm squares
1 red onion, quartered and leaves separated
½ cup sweet chilli sauce
½ cup hot or mild chutney

Cut all the sausages into 2cm pieces. Set aside.

Thread the sticks in the following order: Russian sausage, red pepper, polony, green pepper, Vienna sausage, red or green pepper, onion, and continue until the stick is full. Paint with a little sweet chilli sauce and chutney, then braai over a medium heat, until browned and warmed through.

They really are very impressive when presented.

SERVES 8–10

These cocktail-inspired (but alcohol-free) kebabs are delicious hot or cold.

MOJITO-INSPIRED KEBABS
with fresh mint & herb sauce

a handful fresh origanum, chopped
a few sprigs fresh rosemary, chopped
a handful fresh mint, chopped
4 cloves garlic, crushed
¼ cup lime juice
zest of 1 lime
3 Tbsp honey
2 tsp finely grated fresh ginger
2 Tbsp olive oil
6 chicken kebabs

Mint and herb sauce
1 tsp crushed garlic
½ cup fresh mind leaves, packed
½ cup fresh flat-leaf parsley, packed
2 Tbsp lime juice
½ tsp salt
¼ tsp red chilli flakes
6 Tbsp olive oil

To prepare the marinade, combine the origanum, rosemary, mint, garlic, lime juce and zest, honey, ginger and olive oil in a bowl.

Arrange the chicken kebabs in a rectangular glass dish and pour over the marinade, making sure the kebabs are covered. Leave to marinate for about 2 hours.

Meanwhile, make the herb and mint sauce. Place all the ingredients into the bowl of a food processor and pulse until chopped. (Alternatively, chop everything finely by hand.) Transfer to a small bowl to accompany the kebabs.

When ready, braai, grill or fry the marinated kebabs over a medium heat and serve with the sauce.

MAKES 6

SHARFARI SALADS

A good braai, a great *slaai* – that's what I had in my mind's eye!

Most of the ingredients in these recipes can be grown in your backyard, or in a herb planter. There is nothing more satisfying than growing your own herbs, vegetables and fruit, especially when children and grandchildren plant the first seeds and watch their weekly growth. And the taste of hand-cultivated herbs and plants is incomparable.

Our wonderful weather in South Africa makes a braai with *slaai* (salad in Afrikaans) a Sunday best. People often say to me, 'Don't you find salads are just a variation of lettuce and tomatoes?' My response is that you should NEVER lose the creative will and motivation to make something special with a mere mushroom. I can think of at least 10 wonderful ways with mushrooms, whether grilled with lemon and garlic, marinated in French salad dressing, scattered raw on a salad, grilled and placed onto rocket leaves, grated into a Caesar salad, skewered on a sosatie stick, enjoyed in a pasta, slow cooked in a stew, as a cap on your burger or as a delicious sauce. Mushrooms are magic. You wouldn't want me to start on the care-free, fat-free cabbage now, would you?

More than five ingredients! You're probably asking, 'What am I letting myself in for?'

Believe me, these ingredients just work. My favourite meal is a bagel filled with slightly wet biltong, which I can have in a heartbeat. Need I say more … the heartbeat of this salad is the biltong.

THE HEARTBEAT OF AFRICA SALAD (biltong salad)

1 head butter lettuce, leaves separated and washed
40g rocket
1 avocado, sliced
250g shredded biltong (or more)
250g baby tomatoes
a handful fresh coriander or parsley, off stem
18–20 fresh mint leaves, off stem
a handful fried crispy onions (available at most supermarkets or make your own, see below)

Dressing

½ cup balsamic reduction (see below)
2 Tbsp balsamic vinegar
½ cup canola oil
½ tsp salt

Balsamic reduction

3 cups balsamic vinegar
½ cup brown sugar

Crispy fried onions

2 onions, halved and very thinly sliced
½ cup cornflour
½ tsp paprika
1 tsp salt

First prepare the balsamic reduction (it will make about 2 cups). Mix the balsamic vinegar and brown sugar in a saucepan over a medium heat, stirring constantly until the sugar has dissolved. Bring to the boil, reduce the heat to low, then simmer, uncovered, until reduced by half (20–25 minutes). The reduction should be able to coat the back of a spoon. Leave to cool and pour into a jar with a lid. Store in the refrigerator.

If making your own crispy fried onions (makes about 1–1½ cups), place the onions in a plastic bag, sprinkle with the cornflour, paprika and salt, then seal the bag. Massage the onions until they are evenly coated; they should sweat naturally in the bag, ensuring that the moisture absorbs the flour mixture and coats them. Deep-fry the onions in oil until golden-brown and crispy, then set aside to drain on kitchen paper.

For the dressing, mix the half-cup of balsamic reduction with the vinegar, oil and salt, then whisk until well combined.

To assemble the salad, arrange the lettuce leaves and rocket on a serving platter. Place the avocado slices on top. Sprinkle over the biltong, followed by the tomatoes and coriander or parsley. Place the mint leaves delicately over all. Just before serving, drizzle the dressing over the salad and top with a sprinkling of the crispy fried onions.

SERVES 8–10

It was a relaxed Sunday and I was debating what salads to make when my husband said, 'I really miss my mother's curried rice salad.' Now when a man says that, he's really saying, 'I wish you would make my mother's rice salad, but nobody made it like her.'

Well, I've always been one to enjoy a challenge or, better still, hear his words, 'You know what, my mother's salad was superb but this is different level, Shar!' Or is it that wonderful saying 'happy wife, happy life' that influenced that answer? Dried fruit is a store-cupboard staple, as is rice, but this couldn't be the regular South African curried rice salad, it had to be special, something unique, otherwise how could I have the *chutzpah* to compete with his mother!

Good Old
BROWN RICE AND DRIED FRUIT SALAD

1½ cups brown rice
1 heaped tsp ground turmeric
1 tsp paprika
½ cup finely chopped dried pears
½ cup chopped pitted prunes
¼ cup cranberries
½ cup finely chopped dried apricots
1 small green pepper, chopped
1 medium red onion, finely chopped

Dressing

2 Tbsp Durban curry powder or your favourite curry spice mix
1 Tbsp chicken stock powder
1½–2 cups mayonnaise
2 Tbsp chutney

Make the dressing by combining the ingredients together.

Cook the rice according to the packet instructions, together with the turmeric, paprika, pears, prunes, cranberries and apricots. Once the rice has cooked through, leave to cool, then add the pepper and onion. Pour over the dressing and mix well.

SERVES 8–10

The secret's in the seed! I can hear my son saying, 'Oh no, Ma, not another salad for budgies.' Yes, this is a healthy, seedful salad with the ability to make you whistle like a bird and beg for more.

GREENS AND SEEDS SALAD with ginger dressing

¼ cup sunflower seeds
¼ cup pumpkin seeds
¼ cup sesame seeds
½ cup roughly chopped raw cashew nuts
½ cup chopped raw almonds
½ cup agave or regular syrup
200g baby spinach

Ginger dressing
¼ cup apple cider vinegar
1½ tsp grated fresh ginger
½ tsp chilli flakes
1 Tbsp honey or agave syrup
2 Tbsp sesame oil
⅓ cup canola oil
½ tsp salt

Preheat the oven to 180°C.

Meanwhile, combine the dressing ingredients until well mixed.

Place the seeds and nuts into a bowl and drizzle with the syrup. Mix well, then spread the mixture onto a baking tray. Bake on the middle shelf of the oven for 15 minutes until golden-brown. Remove from the oven and allow to cool before mixing in the baby spinach and drizzling with the dressing.

SERVES 8–10

Africa is a magical place, from its diverse cultures to the warmth of its people and the wonderful array of foods and products. South Africa is a good example of this and one proudly South African brand that captures the warmth, flavour and essence of this dynamic country is the irresistible red piquanté pepper product, bottled under the name of Peppadew. These spicy and sweet peppers were first commercially grown in a small farming industry in Tzaneen.

If you wonder why the ingredients list asks for a butternut with a long neck, it's because the area of the bulb where the pips are housed will not be used.

HARMONY BUTTERNUT SALAD with Peppadew dressing & glazed macon

- 1.5–2kg whole butternut, with a long neck, or 1kg presliced butternut rings
- vegetable oil for drizzling
- dukkah or za'atar spice for sprinkling
- 1 x 400g jar whole Peppadew Mild Piquanté Peppers, with liquid
- 250g hummus
- ½ cup toasted sesame seeds
- 1 x quantity crispy glazed macon (see below)
- a handful fresh coriander or parsley for garnishing

Crispy glazed macon

- 250g beef macon, sliced
- ⅓ cup honey
- 1 Tbsp Dijon mustard

First prepare the macon. Preheat the oven to 180°C. Line 2 baking sheets with baking paper. Arrange the macon slices on the paper in a single layer.

Warm the honey in the microwave or over boiling water in a double boiler on the stove top. Add the mustard and give it a stir to combine well. Paint the mixture over the tops of the macon slices and bake for 10–15 minutes, depending on the thickness and fattiness of the macon, until sizzling and brown. Turn off the oven and leave the macon to crisp until easy to crumble.

Transfer the macon, glazed-side up, to a sheet of brown paper, to drain and cool slightly. (If you place it sticky-side down it will stick to the paper.) Crumble or finely chop the macon, and set aside until ready to use.

To make the salad, preheat the oven to 190°C. Grease an oven tray.

Steam the whole butternut with the skin on for 25 minutes (or the sliced rings for about 12 minutes), just to soften it before baking. When cool, peel the butternut and slice it into thin rings about 0.5cm thick. Arrange the rings in a single layer on the prepared tray, then drizzle them with oil and sprinkle with dukkah or za'atar.

Bake for 30–40 minutes until the edges are a dark golden-brown. Using an egg lifter, turn the butternut rings over and allow to bake on the other side for at least 15 minutes until golden-brown as well.

Meanwhile, blend the Peppadew peppers and liquid, with the hummus in a food processor until smooth.

Remove the butternut from the oven and leave to cool. When ready, arrange the rings on a platter. Just before serving, pour over the dressing and sprinkle with the sesame seeds and macon. Finally, garnish with the coriander or parsley.

SERVES 8

I was in our local fresh fruit and vegetable shop when a young lady walked in, picked up a kohlrabi and exclaimed, 'Now I've seen it all, what on earth is this?' All I could say was it was called a kohlrabi and decided there and then to take some home and experiment. As it was summer I decided it should be used in a fresh salad, and after a few discarded recipes and kohlrabis, we all decided that this version was really crisp, fresh, tasty and easy.

KOHLRABI SLAW to adore

- 3 kohlrabis, thick green flesh peeled away to reveal the light green to white flesh
- 2 crisp firm apples, e.g. Granny Smith, cored
- 6 large red radishes
- 3 cups shredded cabbage, refrigerated
- 2 stalks celery, thinly sliced horizontally
- ⅓ cup dried cranberries
- ¼ cup toasted sesame seeds
- ¼ cup toasted sunflower seeds

Salad dressing

- juice of 2 lemons
- 3 Tbsp sesame oil
- ½ cup sunflower oil
- 3 Tbsp honey
- ½ tsp crushed garlic
- 1 cup mayonnaise
- salt and pepper to taste

First make the salad dressing by placing all the ingredients in a wide-necked bottle or a jar. Shake to combine well.

Shred the kohlrabi, apples and radishes in a food processor with a shredder disc or grate them coarsely. Transfer them to a glass bowl and add the cabbage and celery. Toss gently. then pour over the dressing.

Sprinkle with the cranberries, sesame and sunflower seeds.

SERVES 6–8

Morogo, or *imifino*, is also known as wild or African spinach. I remember asking food anthropologist Anna Trapido how to find it or identify it and she suggested that the best way was to go into a rural area and follow a herdsman foraging for these edible leafy greens. So when our gardener went home for the holidays, he returned with morogo wrapped in wet paper for me to eat and replant. But if you don't have access to that, you may happily replace it with baby spinach leaves.

MOROGO SALAD with pine nut dressing

200g morogo or baby spinach
40–50g rocket
a handful fresh basil leaves
3–4 spring onions, chopped
±15 baby rosa tomatoes
±15 black olives, pitted
200g sliced fresh mushrooms
2 avocados, sliced or chunked

Pine nut dressing
100g toasted pine nuts (reserve 3 Tbsp for garnishing)
3 cloves garlic
¾ cup canola oil
¼ cup white wine vinegar
1 Tbsp prepared grainy mustard
1 Tbsp sugar or sugar-free substitute
salt and pepper to taste

For the dressing, blend the ingredients together until smooth. This makes a delicious, nutty and creamy dressing that should only be poured over lightly just after the avocados are added.

To assemble the salad, arrange all the greens on a platter, followed by the spring onions, tomatoes, olives and mushrooms. Just before serving, add the avocados, pour over the dressing and sprinkle with the reserved pine nuts.

SERVES 10–12

There is something so magical and pure about sitting outside in the fresh air: the tranquility of the trees, birds chirping, a slowly setting sun, the anticipation of evening rain. And then the mood of bliss broken by a 'Are we getting supper tonight? I'm starving!'

OUTDOORS SALAD
with chilli & peanuts

500g minute steak, tenderised and shredded into shuwarma-style strips
3 Tbsp oil
½ cup raw peanuts
1 tsp cayenne pepper or peri-peri powdered spice
1 head butter lettuce
salt and black pepper to taste
6 Israeli cucumbers, julienned
100g fresh peas
250g fresh asparagus (optional)
a handful chopped spring onions

Marinade

3 cloves garlic, crushed
½ cup white vinegar
¼ cup soy sauce
1 Tbsp chopped fresh hot chillies or 1½ tsp dried chilli flakes
2 Tbsp sesame oil
⅔ cup canola oil

To prepare the marinade, whisk the garlic, vinegar, soy sauce, chillies and sesame and canola oils together in a bowl.

Place the steak strips in a Ziploc bag and pour in half the marinade (reserving the rest for the dressing later). Seal the bag and ensure that all of the meat is covered in marinade, then leave to marinate for 1–2 hours.

Remove the meat from the bag and discard any remaining marinade that was in contact with the raw meat. Fry the steaks in the oil over a medium to high heat until lightly browned, but not overdone.

Meanwhile, dry-fry the peanuts in a frying pan for about 3 minutes, tossing until golden-brown and glossy. Transfer the nuts to another bowl and season with the cayenne pepper or peri-peri. Set aside and allow to cool.

Arrange the lettuce on a platter, top with the steak, followed by the cucumbers, peas, asparagus (if using) and spring onions. Drizzle with the reserved marinade and sprinkle over the peanuts.

SERVES 6–8

This is one of my favourite vegetable dishes. As an alternative to room-temperature salad, serve it warm on pasta or, for a dairy option, with grated Parmesan cheese and a wedge of buttered herb focaccia.

ROASTED VEGETABLE SALAD with anchovy dressing

200g salad greens (your choice)
6 baby aubergines, sliced into rounds
1 large bulb fennel, sliced
3 leeks, sliced into 2cm rounds
2 courgettes, sliced into rounds
1 red pepper, deseeded and cut into chunks
1 green pepper, deseeded and cut into chunks
2 small red onions, quartered and leaves separated
¼ cup olive oil
salt and cracked black pepper to taste
a handful olives (optional)

Anchovy dressing
2 Tbsp anchovy paste
3 Tbsp finely chopped fresh flat-leaf parsley
¼ cup lemon juice
½ cup olive oil
1 tsp sugar
2 Tbsp capers

Preheat the oven to 180°C.

Place all the salad greens, aubergines, fennel, leeks, courgettes, red and green peppers and onions into a bowl. Add the oil and season. Mix gently, using your hands.

Spread the vegetables on 1 or 2 roasting trays (don't pile them, otherwise they will steam rather than roast) and roast for about 45 minutes until lightly charred. Meanwhile, combine the dressing ingredients and drizzle over the vegetables after they have roasted. If using, sprinkle over the olives.

SERVES 8–10

This may not be your *bubbe*'s regular recipe for *borscht*, but you could just be the *bubbe* to introduce it so that it continues from generation to generation. A Soweto salad is basically a sliced beetroot salad served at every traditional African wedding and celebration. If there's no beetroot salad, there's something missing! Of course, how you're going to stop it from splashing onto your new outfit is your challenge! Remember to prepare it a day ahead to allow for overnight marinating.

SOWETO SALAD
with bubbe's borscht twist

6 large beetroot, boiled with skins until soft
3 Tbsp olive oil
2 Tbsp chicken stock powder
2 large red onions, sliced
1 tsp salt
¾ cup fresh orange juice
1 cup white vinegar
4 bay leaves
2 Tbsp honey
1 small head red cabbage, shredded
fresh flat-leaf parsley for garnishing

Preheat the oven to 180°C.

Once the beetroot are cool, remove their skins (it's best to wear gloves when peeling them) and cube. Arrange the cubes in a roasting dish, drizzle with the oil and sprinkle over the chicken stock powder. Roast until the edges start to caramelise.

Meanwhile, place the onions, salt, orange juice, vinegar, bay leaves and honey into a bowl and leave to marinate. As soon as the beetroot are roasted, add them to the bowl as well to marinate overnight with the rest.

When ready to serve, arrange the shredded cabbage on a platter followed by the beetroot and onions (removed from the marinade with a slotted spoon). Drizzle with the leftover marinade and garnish with the parsley.

SERVES 8–10

Why sun kissed? Well, the marinade gives the chicken a lovely sunshine orange tinge, and when you love orange lipstick the way I do, then anything I love becomes sunshine kissed.

South Africa is one of the top five citrus producers and exporters in the world. Driving along the open roads towards the Kruger National Park or Sun City – two of our favourite tourist spots – you see acres and acres of orange groves, and there's nothing like a stop at the wonderful farmstalls along the way to freshen up with a glass of just-squeezed orange juice.

Sun-Kissed CHICKEN AND CITRUS SALAD

8 deboned and skinless chicken thighs, cut into thin 1cm x 3cm strips
1 head butter lettuce
50g rocket
1 red onion, very thinly sliced into rings
3 oranges and 1 grapefruit, peeled, segmented and all pith removed
1 bulb fennel, finely sliced
2 avocados, sliced
100g candied pecan nuts

Marinade

3 Tbsp sweet chilli sauce
3 Tbsp Nando's medium-heat chilli sauce
1 tsp finely grated orange zest
juice of 1 orange
1 tsp paprika
1 tsp finely grated fresh ginger
1 Tbsp soy sauce
2 Tbsp sesame oil

Salad dressing

½ cup fresh orange juice
¼ cup fresh lemon juice
¾ cup olive oil
2 Tbsp honey
salt and freshly ground black pepper to taste
1 tsp chopped fresh chilli or ½ tsp dried chilli flakes
1 tsp fennel seeds

Combine all the salad dressing ingredients in a jar and shake until well combined. Make this in advance and leave to absorb all the flavours. Shake well again before serving.

To make the marinade, place all the ingredients in a bowl and whisk until well mixed. Add the chicken strips to the marinade, ensuring that they are evenly coated. Cover and refrigerate for at least 2 hours.

Remove the chicken from the marinade, shaking off any excess (but reserving any leftover marinade). Fry the chicken in a non-stick frying pan until cooked through. Add the leftover marinade to the chicken in the pan and bring to the boil. (This is important as you must avoid any cross contamination from the raw chicken that was in the marinade). Once boiled, set aside to cool.

Arrange the lettuce and rocket on a platter. Place the chicken, onion rings, oranges, grapefruit, fennel and avocados on top. Just before serving, drizzle with the salad dressing and sprinkle over the pecan nuts.

SERVES 8–10

Chakalaka is considered to be a salad in Soweto, but think of it as a spicy vegetable relish because the vegetables are chopped and cooked. I created this recipe for a themed Shabbat lunch that infused Asian, African and Indian flavours. The first time I made it, I served it with brown sugar beans, but it wasn't until I created it as a deconstructed sushi salad that it flew off the platter. When I asked my domestic helper what the isiZulu or isiXhosa word for 'deconstructed' is, she responded quite simply, 'Do you mean it's broken?' Well yes, that's exactly what it is, so it became *tsebrochen* (Yiddish for 'broken') salad. If you need to save time, you can prepare the chakalaka sauce a day ahead or use a readymade one.

TSEBROCHEN SALAD (deconstructed chakalaka sushi salad)

3 cups ready-cooked sushi rice, or 3 x 85g vegetable-flavoured Ramen noodles
1 English cucumber, pith removed and julienned
250g baby mealies, sliced on the diagonal
250g sugar snap peas, sliced on the diagonal
1 red pepper, deseeded and thinly sliced
1 green pepper, deseeded and thinly sliced
1 yellow pepper, deseeded and thinly sliced
2 carrots, julienned
½ cup chopped spring onions
100g salted cashew nuts
a handful chopped fresh coriander for garnishing

Dressing

½ cup chakalaka sauce (page 194 or readymade)
1 cup mayonnaise
½ cup cold water
½ cup white wine vinegar
2 tsp sugar or sweetener

If using the Ramen noodles instead of sushi rice, prepare the noodles according to the packet instructions, but retain the third packet for crumbling the dry noodles over the salad.

Spoon the sushi rice or noodles onto a platter and cover with the cucumber, mealies, peas, peppers, carrots and spring onions. Alternatively, arrange the ingredients in groups over the rice.

To make the dressing, combine the chakalaka with the mayonnaise, water, vinegar and sugar or sweetener until well mixed.

When ready to serve, pour the dressing over the sushi rice and vegetables and garnish with the cashew nuts and fresh coriander. If using noodles, crumble the third packet of noodles over the top of the dressed salad.

SERVES 8–10

Walking around my garden a while back, looking for my grandson's tennis ball, I came across what looked like a gorgeous Fabergé egg. It was, in fact, a giant aubergine (also known as eggplant or brinjal) lying gently amongst the plants. And there were more. I brought in some wooden stakes (as aubergines need height and support) and hopefully my horticultural skills, of which I have less than zero, will be rewarded with a bumper crop for this delicious salad. The idea is to create the appearance of petals on a flower using 12 aubergine shell halves arranged on a round platter. If you like, you could prepare the falafel crumb mix 2–3 days ahead of time.

AFRICAN AUBERGINE PETAL SALAD with techina dressing & falafel crumbs

6 medium aubergines
olive oil for rubbing and frying
1 x 180g packet Osem falafel mix
2–2½ cups cold water
2 onions, chopped
1 tsp crushed garlic
salt and pepper to taste
½ cup mayonnaise
a handful fresh coriander, finely chopped
a handful fresh mint, finely chopped
1 x 250g tub hummus
1 x 250g tub techina sauce mixed with ½ cup cold water

Preheat the oven to 180°C.

Arrange the aubergines in a roasting dish, prick their skins and rub them with a little oil. Roast whole for 40 minutes.

Meanwhile, make the falafel crumbs. Place the mix in a bowl and add the cold water (NOT 1 cup as stated on the packet, because it should be a rather loose batter). Pour oil 1cm up the sides of a frying pan and heat to a medium to high heat. Pour half the batter into the pan and fry until golden-brown and crisp. Mix it about while frying to prevent it from sticking together in a clump. If some bits cling together while frying, don't worry as you'll be able to break them down once cool. Remove from the pan with a slotted spoon and drain on kitchen or brown paper. Repeat with the other half of the batter.

Remove the aubergines from the oven, allow to cool, then cut in half lengthwise. Scoop out the flesh with a spoon, leaving the skins intact. (Don't worry if the flesh is still a little hard as it will be fried.)

Fry the onions in a little oil, along with the garlic and aubergine flesh, until soft. Season to taste, then remove from the heat and leave to cool in a bowl. Add the mayonnaise, coriander, mint and hummus.

Turn the oven onto grill and return the aubergine shells to the roasting dish, skin-side down. Place them under the griller and allow them to brown up. Remove from the oven and leave to cool. Once cool, fill the shells (or petals) with the aubergine flesh mixture.

Drizzle the techina sauce over the filled petals and, just before serving, sprinkle them with the falafel crumbs. You could also serve this unusual salad with baked tortilla wraps. Paint the tortillas with a little oil, sprinkle over some garlic salt and bake them at 180°C for approximately 20 minutes until golden-brown. Turn off the heat and leave them to crisp in the oven. Allow to cool before serving.

SERVES 10–12

A delicious light lunch served at tables covered with crisp white tablecloths in a vineyard in Stellenbosch where the grapes hang in perfect manicured lines waiting to be harvested and (hopefully) turned into the wine of the month or year ... these are the dreams of the vintner. The wineries in South Africa stand proud as some of the best in the world and their vineyards play host to many a wedding, celebration or lunch. At a recent *simcha* (celebration) I had the opportunity to taste a Cape vineyard's special snoek salad with a glass of fabulous wine. If you like, you could substitute the snoek with smoked trout or salmon.

Vineyard SMOKED SNOEK SALAD

100g fresh rocket
100g watercress or mixed salad greens
250–300g smoked snoek, flaked and deboned
1 cup seedless white grapes
1 cup seedless red grapes
200g fresh asparagus, cooked *al dente*
4 boiled eggs, halved
1 red onion, sliced very thinly into rings
100g bean sprouts

Dressing
1 cup mayonnaise
2 Tbsp wholegrain mustard
3 large sweet 'n sour pickled cucumbers, finely grated
¼ cup liquid from pickled cucumbers
2 Tbsp honey
salt and pepper to taste

First make the dressing by mixing all the ingredients until well combined.

Arrange the rocket and watercress on a platter followed by the fish, grapes, asparagus, eggs, onion rings and sprouts. Just before serving, drizzle the dressing over the salad.

Serve with seed crackers such as the ultimate health crackers (page 36).

SERVES 6–8

MENCHABLES – WHAT A GREAT BUNCH

Vegetables add colour, not only to a plate, but to the land as well. When flying in or out of the coast of Durban and peering out of the aircraft window, you can see the beautifully contoured lines of vegetation flowing through the hills and valleys. It is a sight to behold, like a perfectly combed zen garden in a landscape of abundant colour. Rich green sugar cane plantations, corn fields, and banana and avocado trees vie with intermittent ploughed areas waiting patiently to be planted to prove their fertililty. As you travel in a south-westerly direction, the vegetable crops of the Garden Route beckon en route to the Cape winelands and the golden fields of wheat of the Swartland.

The bunny chow was invented to beat the system during apartheid South Africa, which dictated a whites-only clientele in Durban's sit-down restaurants. Café owners opened up hatch windows for other customers, and devised an ingenious edible package for their takeaways: the meal, crockery and cutlery were all in one. Curries were served in hollowed-out, half-loaves of bread, topped with a 'lid' made from the scooped-out bread. Bunnies are filled with curried meat or vegetables, the recipes for which were brought to South Africa by indentured Indian labourers who came to work in the sugar-cane fields of KwaZulu-Natal. Bunnies are always eaten bare-handed, starting with the soft lid on top; breaking pieces off and using them to mop up the curry inside. Thereafter one pulls the bread, piece by piece, from the sides in a concentric circle, spiralling downwards to keep mopping up. Oh yes, the name – 'bunny' derives from *bania*, the ethnic group of Indian businessmen who sold the bunnies, and 'chow', of course, is slang for food. This bunny, filled with curried vegetables, mixed veg sambals and some pickles is so good!

Veggie BUNNY CURRY

---

1 large onion, sliced
200g green beans, cut into 1cm pieces
2 hot green chillies, seeded and chopped
¼ cup cooking oil
1 x 400g can chopped Italian tomatoes
½ tsp ground turmeric
½ tsp ground coriander
½ tsp ground cumin
1 tsp curry or chilli powder
1 tsp finely grated fresh ginger
1 tsp crushed garlic
2 large potatoes, cubed
½ cup water
salt to taste
1 x 400g can lentils
1 x 400g can cannellini beans
1 whole white government bread, halved

In a large pan, fry the onion and green beans, together with the chillies, in the oil until soft. Add the tomatoes and fry for a further 2–3 minutes. Stir in the turmeric, coriander, cumin, curry or chilli powder, ginger, garlic, potatoes, water and salt. Finally, add the lentils and beans (in their sauce) and allow to simmer for about 30 minutes until some of the liquid reduces. Cover the pan and leave the curry to rest, to absorb all the wonderful flavours.

You are now ready to fill your scooped out half-loaves of bread for a memorable bunny! If, however, you'd prefer something a little more 'elegant', you could use the curry as filling in miniature loaves or bread rolls.

MAKES ENOUGH TO FILL 4 HALF-LOAVES OR 10–12 BREAD ROLLS (DEPENDING ON SIZE)

In the times of the Temple, oil that should have lasted only 1 day miraculously lasted 8, so it is customary to eat foods fried in oil over this period to symbolise this miracle. The festival of lights, which is anything but 'lite' calorie wise, allows us to eat all the lovely fried food without any guilt.

Chanukkah normally falls over our summer holiday, towards the end of the year, so we often combine Chanukkah with an end-of-year party. It gives me the opportunity to take out the deep-fryers and frying pans for *latkes*, fat cakes, doughnuts, *slap* chips and chilli bites (*dahltjies*, pronounced dull-keys or daaaarrlingkies as one of my friends calls them).

Cape Malay culture has significantly influenced South Africa's wide variety of culinary delights and *dhaltjies* are often served as an accompaniment to curries. They may vary a little in texture and flavour from person to person, but they are delicious darling!

CAPE MALAY DAAAARRLINGKIES (chilli bites)

1 cup chick pea flour
1½ cups cake flour
1 onion, very finely chopped or grated
250g baby spinach leaves, finely shredded
2 tsp crushed dried chillies
1 tsp red masala
1 tsp salt
1 tsp ground turmeric
1 tsp ground coriander
1 tsp ground cumin
water
sunflower oil for deep-frying
1 tsp baking powder

Sift the flours into a large bowl. Mix in the onion, spinach, chillies, masala, salt, turmeric, coriander and cumin. Add enough water to make a thick batter (it mustn't be runny).

Heat the oil in a deep frying pan until fairly hot. Stir the baking powder into the batter just before frying. Using a tablespoon, drop the batter into the oil and fry slowly until golden-brown. (Ensure that the oil doesn't get too hot, otherwise the chilli bites will burn on the outside and remain raw in the middle.) Test by piercing with a toothpick. If it comes out dry, the chilli bites are ready. Remove from the heat and drain on absorbent kitchen paper.

Serve warm.

MAKES 20

The best golden-brown, crispy, tasty, latke to ever accompany any meal, whether breakfast, lunch or supper. I can't say much more about these other than once you start you can't stop, just like popcorn, oy, there I go trying to be corny again!

CHAKALAKA CORN LATKES (FRITTERS) with avocado aïoli sauce

3 cups frozen corn kernels, defrosted
6 Tbsp chakalaka (readymade or page 194)
1 large potato, grated
1 chilli, finely chopped (optional)
1 cup cake flour, sifted
1 egg
1 tsp baking powder
salt and pepper to taste
cooking oil for frying

Avocado aïoli sauce
½ cup mashed avocado
1 Tbsp lemon juice
1 tsp crushed garlic
½ cup mayonnaise

First make the avocado aïoli sauce by combining all the ingredients.

In a bowl, combine the corn kernels, chakalaka, potato, chilli (if using), flour, egg, baking powder and salt and pepper.

Heat oil in a frying pan over a medium heat, then drop heaped spoonfuls of batter into the oil. As the *latkes* fry, flatten them slightly with the back of the spoon. Once they are golden-brown and crispy, drain them on kitchen or brown paper.

Serve with the sauce.

MAKES ±14

The year 2010 created an unprecedented amount of World Cup soccer fever in South Africa. Street food was out in its full glory, as were the vuvuzelas. This plastic horn, about 65cm long, produces a loud, annoying monotone, which my husband loves. He says it brings an African feel and a wonderful vibe to the stadiums. I think they used spoons in Russia to create a similar atmosphere, as vuvuzelas have been banned in some countries. Spoons seem a more appropriate option, well for me anyway. I remember walking through the streets on the way to one of the matches, and being struck by the wonderful smell of boerewors puffing through the air and the unmistakable aroma of curry weaving its way in between. Samoosas are small pastry parcels (often triangular in shape) with a delicious curry filling. There's nothing quite as magnificent as the tastes of our rainbow cuisine.

VUVUZELA SAMOOSAS

1 x 500g phyllo pastry
2 x 400g cans curried vegetables
2 Tbsp cake flour
3 Tbsp water
olive oil spray

Preheat the oven to 180°C.

Place 2 sheets of phyllo pastry on top of each other and cut into 4 double pieces of pastry. Cover the rest of the phyllo pastry with a damp cloth.

Spoon some of the vegetables onto each 'stack' of phyllo in a diagonal line (2cm wide and 7cm long) across the bottom left-hand corner. Start rolling the pastry, keeping the bottom tight so that it looks like a long cone.

Mix the flour and water to form a paste. With your finger, paint some of it along the top of the cone and fold a piece over the top to seal it. Repeat until you've used up all the vegetables. Spray each samoosa with olive oil. Arrange all the samoosas on a baking tray and bake for 15 minutes until golden-brown. Turn them over and bake for another 10 minutes until golden-brown. Remember, the vegetables are already cooked so it's just to make them crispy.

MAKES 12

Pumpkin is one of South Africa's favourite vegetables. Even most restaurants serve pumpkin and spinach as vegetable side dishes with main meals. This recipe is an infusion of two cultures – a traditional Jewish pumpkin *kugel* with traditional South African pumpkin bread pudding, known as *pampoenmoes*. People who generally don't like pumpkin often make an exception for this delicious dish.

PAMPOENMOES (pumpkin babke)

1kg pumpkin, cubed (2 x 2cm)
butter or margarine for spreading
8 slices cinnamon *babke* or bread, sliced 1cm thick and crusts removed
¼ cup brown sugar
2 tsp ground cinnamon (4 tsp if using plain bread instead of cinnamon *babke*)
½ tsp ground cardamom
½ tsp ground ginger
4 eggs
2 cups 'lite' coconut milk or soya milk
1 cup water

Preheat the oven to 170°C. Grease an ovenproof dish.

Boil the pumpkin until soft. Mash lightly with a fork (it still needs a little texture).

Lightly butter both sides of the bread, then slice into 2cm cubes. Mix the sugar and cinnamon together. Arrange a layer of buttered bread in the dish, then follow this with a layer of pumpkin. Sprinkle liberally with the cinnamon-sugar mixture. Repeat, ending with a final layer of bread.

Beat the eggs, milk and water together and pour over the pumpkin and bread layers. Allow the bread to absorb the custard mixture, pressing it down with the back of a spoon.

Bake in the oven until the dish starts to bubble and the top is crispy, but not burnt (25–30 minutes).

Serve as a side dish to meat.

SERVES 8

The impressive King Protea is the national flower of South Africa and has become very popular in flower arrangements, including wedding flowers. I recently received a bunch of these proteas as a Shabbos gift, and because they lasted so long, I had enough time to study them well. Their open-leaved head of petals with an almost beefy appearance reminded me of the popular 'fried blooming onion'. And so this national symbol of our country, which lends its name to many of our sports teams, became the motivation for this recipe.

Blooming Protea FRIED ONION

1 large onion
¼ cup self-raising flour
salt to taste
1 tsp cayenne pepper
1 egg
¾ cup cold water
oil for deep-frying

Peel the onion, but keep most of the root or base end intact. Cut the top of the onion off, about 1cm deep. Using a small, sharp knife, cut away and scoop out the centre of the onion, about three-quarters of the way down, just removing the centre core – almost the amount an apple corer would remove from an apple, i.e. 1cm diameter, but not all the way through to the root. Immerse the onion in a bowl of ice-cold water until the leaves 'blossom' and open.

Pour the flour, salt and cayenne pepper into a Ziploc bag, giving it a good shake. Add the onion to the bag and shake well to coat each petal with as much flour as possible.

Beat the egg and cold water together in a small bowl, large enough to house the onion. Dip the flour-coated onion into the egg mixture, ensuring that each leaf is well covered. Sprinkle the remaining flour in the bag over the onion, and dip the onion back into the egg mixture.

Heat oil in a deep frying pan over a medium to high heat, so that the oil bubbles up rapidly as you immerse the onion. Carefully lower the onion into the hot oil, then reduce the heat to make sure that it cooks all the way through (5–7 minutes) until golden-brown and crisp. Watch it all the time as it can burn quickly. Remove the onion from the pan and leave to drain upside-down on kitchen paper for a few minutes.

Serve with a dipping sauce, such as sweet chilli sauce or cucumber relish* and non-dairy sour cream, or regular sour cream if you're going the dairy route. Serve immediately or keep in a warm oven (110°C), uncovered, so that it remains crispy, but definitely not longer than 30–40 minutes.

*Finely grate 3 sweet and sour pickled cucumbers. Dissolve 2 teaspoons of cornflour (e.g. Maizena) in 1 cup of cold pickle juice and 2 teaspoons of sugar in a small saucepan. Bring to the boil, whisking all the time. Finally, add the grated cucumber, mix well and set aside to cool, then refrigerate. This also makes a wonderful relish for burgers.

Serves 2

DELI AND STREET FOOD

This may well be my favourite chapter. Both deli and street foods say, 'Tasty, convenient, easy, quick.' The *delikatessen* evolved in 18th-century Germany, from where emigrants, often the Ashkenazi, took the concept to North America and other countries. The word 'delicatessen' was ultimately whittled down to 'deli' in everyday parlance. Most delicatessens sell delicious cold meats, sandwiches such as hot beef on rye, salads, bagels with cream cheese and lox, *latkes*, chicken soup, *kneidlach* and pickles.

Street food prepared and sold by the locals is probably one of the best and most authentic ways to experience the culture and people of a country, and is usually inexpensive. Whether *amagwinya* (fat cakes), kotas, Gatsbys, bunny chows, braaied mealies or boerewors rolls, the street foods of South Africa are so delicious that upmarket restaurants are taking great pride in serving these treats. Because most require no cutlery, it makes eating 'on the go' so easy. You will find street vendors selling food at taxi ranks, bus stops, railway stations and high-density areas near office blocks.

For some exciting twists on tradition and taste,
Try these recipes, they won't go to waste
Vetkoek, *tshotlô* or chopped liver on a plate,
You can even use your hands – *Es Gezunterheit*.

Every South African claims to have the best *frikkadel* (meatball) recipe. These vary, often according to heritage, so they could incorporate a little cumin and coriander, or have rice in the mixture. On occasion, I've even added some boerewors mince to my beef mixture.

However, there are a few basic rules to a great meatball. The meat needs fat, as pure beef makes them too hard. Use binders such as breadcrumbs (or my favourite – salty crackers) and eggs. Don't overwork the mixture and don't overcook it, but ensure that the meatballs have a golden-brown crust. Once rolled into shape, they should be refrigerated for at least 40 minutes, as that prevents them from falling apart during cooking.

WHAT THE FRIKKADEL?

1kg beef mince
2 large onions, finely chopped
2 tsp crushed garlic
½ cup finely chopped fresh parsley
2 eggs, lightly beaten
2 cups finely crushed Salticrax or similar salty crackers
½ cup cold water
½ tsp grated nutmeg
20g tomato paste
a pinch salt
cooking oil for frying

Sauce
2 x 400g cans chopped tomatoes
½ cup hot chutney
salt and pepper to taste
1 tsp crushed garlic
1 tsp finely chopped fresh chilli
1 tsp sugar

Combine the mince, onions, garlic, parsley, eggs, crackers, water, nutmeg, tomato paste and salt. Roll into golf ball-sized balls. Heat oil in a frying pan and fry the balls, a few at a time, until golden-brown. (If you overcrowd the pan, the balls will boil rather than turn golden-brown.) Once the meatballs have all been fried, set aside.

Meanwhile, combine all the sauce ingredients in a saucepan and bring to the boil over a medium to high heat. Lower the heat and allow the sauce to simmer for 20 minutes, with the lid lying loosely on top. Place the meatballs into the tomato sauce and simmer for a further 10 minutes.

Serve with *mieliepap*, rice, polenta or mashed potatoes.

MAKES 16 MEATBALLS

Qixiang chef industry Ltd.

Biltong has been part of the South African culinary landscape for centuries. Some say this dried meat is more addictive than crisps and nuts. What can this delicacy be compared to? Nothing! It's in a class of its own. It may be enjoyed on its own as an appetiser or as an all-day munch. Taking a piece of biltong away from a teething baby is like trying to take a bone away from a dog. You may get bitten – even if the baby only has one tooth!

Homemade biltong must be one of the most satisfying, rewarding and appreciated meat products you can create. And it's quite normal to experiment a few times before you hear: 'This is the best batch you've ever made!' And that recipe will become your best-kept secret.

Although it may seem that you are buying quite a lot of meat to make biltong because it dehydrates and reduces to half its original weight, after tasting it you may just wish you'd bought more!

BILTONG

6kg beef (e.g. top round, round bolo, shoulder bolo, eye of round)
250g coarse salt
½ cup brown sugar
1 Tbsp bicarbonate of soda
1½ tsp ground black pepper
½ cup dried coriander seeds, coarsely ground
½ cup brown vinegar, decanted into a spray bottle
1 cup water
1 cup red wine vinegar

Cutting along the natural dividing lines of the muscles and always *with* the grain, cut the meat into strips about 2.5cm thick and any desired length.

Mix the salt, sugar, bicarbonate of soda, pepper and coriander together. Rub the mixture thoroughly into the strips of meat. Layer the meat, with the bulkier pieces at the bottom, in a glass or plastic container, spraying the brown vinegar over each layer as you add them. Leave the meat in a cool place for 12 hours or longer (depending on how salty you prefer it), then remove from the marinade.

Mix the water and red wine vinegar and dip the strips of meat into it. This makes the biltong shiny and dark. Once this is complete, the biltong is ready to dry. Pat the strips of meat dry, then hang them on S-shaped hooks, or use pieces of string, about 5cm apart, in a cool to warm, dry area with an oscillating fan blowing over them. It is very important that the air is dry, because too much moisture will cause the meat to spoil. Biltong boxes are also available to purchase and there are websites that will show you how to make your own.

The biltong is ready when the outside is hard and the centre is still a little moist. Let the centre dry according to personal taste.

Cut the biltong from the 'stick', against the grain, into thin pieces using a very sharp knife.

MAKES ±3KG

I love noshing on popcorn, especially macon-flavoured popcorn. If you can't find macon, you could sprinkle shredded and finely chopped smoked brisket over the popcorn.

Macon-Flavoured POPCORN

250g macon
2 Tbsp oil
⅓ cup popcorn kernels
salt to taste

In a deep, 30cm saucepan, fry the macon in the oil over a medium to high heat for about 5 minutes until lightly browned and crispy. Remove from the saucepan and set aside.

If it appears that the meat absorbed all the oil, add another 2 or 3 tablespoons of oil to the saucepan and add the popcorn. (Remember the saucepan must be large enough to allow the kernels to pop comfortably.) When the popping starts, keep shaking the saucepan by the handles to prevent the popped kernels from burning. Once the popping slows down, the popcorn is ready.

Remove from the stove top, sprinkle with a little salt, crumble over the crispy macon and mix well.

MAKES 7–8 CUPS

That is exactly what's hidden inside these crispy, crumbed balls. Fried chopped liver! You can use readymade chopped liver or make your own. And don't forget the onions – that's the secret!

What Am I – CHOPPED LIVER?

¼ cup oil or *schmaltz* (page 87)
3 large onions, chopped
1 tsp sugar
250–300g ready-grilled kosher chicken livers
2 tsp chicken stock powder
3 hard-boiled eggs
salt and pepper to taste
½ cup breadcrumbs or cornflake crumbs

Coating

1 beaten egg mixed with 2 Tbsp water
1 cup breadcrumbs or cornflake crumbs
canola oil for deep-frying

Dipping sauce

3 Tbsp bottled red chrain (horseradish in beetroot dye
6 Tbsp mayonnaise

Heat the oil or *schmaltz* in a large pot and fry the onions and sugar until golden-brown. (Caramelising the onions is the secret to that special-tasting liver.) Remove the pot from the heat once the onions are browned.

Wash the chicken livers in cold water and remove any burnt bits, membranes and sinew. Add the livers to the onions and mix well until all the livers are well coated with onions and oil. Sprinkle over the chicken stock powder. Heat through and scrape all the bits off the bottom of the pot (that's where the flavour is).

Mince the liver and onions with the boiled eggs, using a hand or electric mincer. Add salt and pepper to taste. (For a smoother texture, divide the mixture in half, then mince one half again and mix it with the remaining half. If you prefer it even smoother, blend all in a food processor until it reaches a pâté-like texture.) Add the half cup of breadcrumbs (over Passover you can use matzah meal), allow to cool, then refrigerate immediately. This is very important as the mixture should be very firm. Once firm, divide the liver mixture into balls just smaller than a golf ball.

When ready to cook, dip the balls into the beaten egg mixture and then coat them in the breadcrumbs (or matzah meal over Passover).

In a frying pan, heat oil to a medium to high heat and deep-fry the balls until golden-brown. Remember, the filling is already cooked so it's only necessary to crisp the liver balls on the outside. Remove and set aside to drain on kitchen paper.

Meanwhile, make the dipping sauce by combining the red chrain and mayonnaise.

Serve the balls at room temperature with the dipping sauce.

MAKES 15 BALLS

Kotas are undeniably one of the most famous street foods of South Africa. They are usually filled with polony, atchar and slap chips, and topped with an optional layer of sauce, egg and meat. Here is my version of this three-in-one meal.

KOSHER KOTA

1 loaf regular government bread, halved vertically and horizontally into quarters
500g chopped liver (home- or readymade)
4 Russian sausages, grilled then halved
8 slices polony (with or without garlic), cut 0.5cm thick and lightly fried
12 slices pastrami
16 *slap* chips
BBQ sauce (your favourite readymade brand)
4 fried eggs (optional)
4 Tbsp atchar (your favourite flavour)

Scoop out the soft bread centres from the quarter-loaves. Smear some chopped liver over the base and sides of each hollowed bread. Divide the sausages, polony, pastrami and chips equally among the quarter loaves and fill their hollows. Pour the BBQ sauce over each, and place an egg on top (if using), followed by a tablespoon of atchar.

MAKES 4

We hadn't seen rain for about 2 months and gardens generally looked sad and dusty. My gardener said, 'Don't worry about the garden. When we put up your tent with the palm leaves, the rain will come!' He was right, it always rains over Sukkot in South Africa, making table laying rather tricky. But the traditional delicious wrapped foods, symbolic of us wrapped in the temporary walls of the sukkah, taste even better when accompanied by rain – blessings all the way.

It's Raining DELI WRAPS

6 flour tortillas or wraps
½ cup readymade pesto (e.g. basil)
½ cup mayonnaise
1 tsp hot sauce
35g fresh rocket
6 deboned and cooked chicken breasts, shredded

Place the wraps in aluminium foil and warm them in the oven until soft (this makes it easier to roll them when filled).

Combine the pesto with the mayonnaise and hot sauce. Smear the mixture over each warm wrap. Sprinkle over some rocket and then cover with shredded chicken. Roll each wrap up tightly and slice into 3cm pieces.

Arrange on a platter and garnish as desired, e.g. strips of cucumber, grated carrots or flat-leaf parsley. The wraps are best on the day they're made.

MAKES 6

Just when we thought that the delis of New York had created this incredible dish with pull-apart brisket, out of the woodwork comes *tshotlô* (Setswana, referring to shredded beef), a favourite traditional dish going back centuries! Here's the one that worked for the Lurie family jury.

TSHOTLÔ SANDWICH (pulled beef)

2kg fresh brisket
baguette, rye bread or ciabatta rolls for serving

Rub

3 tsp paprika
2 tsp ground cinnamon
1 Tbsp mustard powder
1 tsp garlic powder
1 tsp chilli powder
1 tsp ground coriander
1 tsp garlic powder (?already listed above, or should it be 2 tsp in total?)
½ tsp salt
1 tsp crushed pepper

Sauce

1 cup apple juice
1 heaped Tbsp grainy prepared mustard
½ cup soft brown sugar
1 cup tomato ketchup
1 tsp chilli flakes

To prepare the rub, mix all the ingredients in a bowl. Massage the rub into the brisket and refrigerate the meat, covered, overnight.

Preheat the oven to 160°C.

For the sauce, combine all the ingredients. Place the pre-rubbed brisket into a roasting pan and pour over the sauce. Tightly cover the entire roasting pan with 2 layers of aluminium foil and gently steam the meat in the oven for 4–5 hours, until tender.

Remove the foil covering the pan, increase the heat to 220°C and roast the meat, uncovered, for 20–30 minutes, until golden-brown. Once done, transfer the meat to a large platter, reserving the juices in the bottom of the roasting pan. Using 2 forks, shred the brisket. Pour the sauce from the roasting pan over the meat and toss lightly.

Serve in a baguette, on rye or in ciabatta rolls, with coleslaw on the side.

MAKES 6–7 SANDWICHES

Whether you call them *magwinya* (Setswana), *pontschkes* (Yiddish), Yorkshire puddings with a twist or *vetkoek* (Afrikaans), these small, unsweetened balls of deep-fried dough can be given sweet or savoury fillings. Well-loved favourites include butter and jam, syrup, minced beef curry, curried vegetables and cheese. I've been known to fill them with peri-peri chicken livers and chopped liver! These traditional South African treats are enjoyed by many local cultures, not just in Afrikaans homes. *Magwinya* are sold in townships at just about every taxi rank and bus stop to commuters on their way to and from work. This is how I love to serve them.

VETKOEK WITH ROAST BEEF
& onion marmalade

4 large onions, halved and thinly sliced
oil for frying
2 Tbsp brown sugar
1 cup red wine
750g sliced rare roast beef

Dough
2 cups cake flour
½ tsp salt
7g fast-acting dried yeast
275–300ml water
3 cups cooking oil

Fry the onions in oil until lightly golden in colour. Add the sugar and keep stirring until it has dissolved. Pour in the wine and bring to the boil. Lower the heat and allow the sauce to reduce and thicken to a delicious marmalade, then leave to cool.

To make the dough, combine the flour, salt and yeast in a large bowl. Add the water, a little at a time, mixing with a wooden spoon until a wet dough forms. Knead in the bowl for 5 minutes or until the dough springs back after being pressed with your finger. Cover the bowl with clingfilm and allow the dough to rise for 30–45 minutes, or until doubled in size.

Divide the dough into 10–12 equal portions (just a bit bigger than golf balls) and leave to double in size before frying (this will keep them light).

As the *vetkoek* need deep-frying, heat the oil in a deep saucepan or pan. Once the oil is hot, reduce the heat to medium, then gently drop 4 *vetkoek* into the oil and cover the saucepan or pan with a lid. This allows the *vetkoek* to partially steam while frying. Fry for 2 minutes, or until golden on one side, then turn and cook the other side. Once cooked through and golden, remove the *vetkoek* from the oil with a slotted spoon and drain on kitchen paper. Repeat with the remaining *vetkoek*.

Slice the *vetkoek* through the middle and fill with the sliced beef. Spread the marmalade over the beef, or serve on the side for dipping.

MAKES 10–12

The popular Gatsby sandwich from the Mother City, Cape Town, can be compared to the Johannesburg kota. This mother of all sandwiches is believed to have been inspired by F. Scott Fitzgerald's famous novel, *The Great Gatsby*, due to its association with 'excess'. A Gatsby is essentially a long sandwich filled with various ingredients. Most typically hot *slap* chips form the base. Thereafter the choice of ingredients ranges from sausages, polony, steak and eggs to bean sprouts and avocado. You can enjoy a greasy fry-up or go as healthy and creative as you feel.

The Beefiest Great Gatsby SANDWICH IN TOWN

2 Tbsp ground cumin
1 tsp salt
1 tsp cracked black pepper
1kg minute steaks, finely sliced, or ask your butcher to cut it shuwarma-style
½ cup techina paste mixed as per instructions on bottle or readymade techina sauce
2 large pickled cucumbers, grated and drained
1 French baguette
6 butter lettuce leaves

Green coleslaw

½ head green cabbage, finely shredded
3 stalks celery, finely sliced
⅓ cup olive oil
juice of 2 lemons
2 Tbsp white sugar or sweetener
1 tsp crushed fresh garlic
1 tsp salt

First make the coleslaw by combining all the ingredients, ensuring the cabbage is well coated. Set aside for about 20 minutes to absorb all the flavours and reduce in size to a nicely coated cabbage salad.

Sprinkle the cumin, salt and pepper over the steaks and rub all in well. Fry the steaks over a high heat until they are cooked through.

Combine the techina sauce and grated cucumbers, then set aside.

Slice the baguette in half lengthwise, hollowing out some of the bread from the crust. Spread the techini pickle relish over both cut sides. Place the lettuce on either side of the baguette. Top with the meat, followed by the coleslaw.

Bite into that and enjoy the greatest Gatsby ever!

SERVES 4

Easy to mash, make in a flash! These puffs can be served as a starter or a side. And they're so delicious; whenever I offer to bring something for supper or lunch, people always say 'Biltong puffs, please!' As they should be eaten as shortly after frying as possible, if I'm taking them elsewhere, I warm them, uncovered, in the oven to crisp at 180°C for 5–10 minutes.

BILTONG PUFFS & chilanaise sauce

250g finely shredded biltong
3–4 large potatoes
½ cup potato flour
2 eggs, lightly beaten
1 cup breadcrumbs or cornflake crumbs seasoned with salt and pepper to taste
cooking oil for frying

Chilanaise sauce
¾ cup mayonnaise
¼ cup favourite chilli sauce (I use Nando's medium heat)

First make the chilanaise sauce by combining the mayonnaise and chilli sauce.

If the biltong isn't fine enough, pulse it in a food processor a few times until almost as fine as biltong dust.

Boil the potatoes in their jackets as there shouldn't be any excess water in the mashed potato. When soft (test with a toothpick), remove them from the water, allow to cool and peel away the skins. Mash or push through a potato ricer and mix together with the shredded biltong and potato flour. Roll into golf ball-sized balls and flatten slightly. Dip them first in the beaten egg, then into the seasoned crumbs.

Heat cooking oil in a pan and fry the puffs until golden-brown, then leave to drain on kitchen or brown paper. Serve with the chilanaise sauce.

MAKES ±24

My granddaughter Zahara loves the kitchen and I love cooking with her. Her *slaptjips* (pronounced 'slup chips') are the best and involve no deep frying, only lightly oiled baking. They're crisp on the outside and soft in the centre.

Zahara's SLAPTJIPS

6 large unpeeled potatoes
1 cup cooking oil
1 Tbsp paprika
salt and vinegar to taste

Microwave the potatoes on high for 15 minutes or boil them for 20–25 minutes, to soften a little. Allow to cool, then peel. Slice them lengthwise, about 1cm thick.

Preheat the oven to 180°C.

Place the potato slices in a large bowl and add the oil and paprika. Toss well to ensure they are well covered, then transfer to a baking sheet and bake until golden-brown and crispy. Enjoy with salt and vinegar.

SERVES 6

Curried fish has to be one of the most popular fish dishes in South Africa. Traditionally, when we make fish balls and fried fish for the Jewish holidays, we tend to go a little overboard, 'just in case we don't have enough!' So leftover fried fish is always a given. At least that eases the pain of wastage. If you don't have any leftover fish, well done!

The easiest way to make this dish if you don't have any leftover fish is to buy readymade fried fish pieces or fish balls and enjoy this Cape Malay version of curried fish. The longer it soaks in the sauce, the tastier it becomes.

Curried CAPE MALAY FISH

oil for frying
3 large onions, sliced into rings
1 Tbsp finely grated fresh ginger
4 cloves garlic, crushed
2–4 red hot chillies (depends how hot you like it), chopped
12–15 whole black peppercorns
4 whole cloves
4 allspice berries
4 bay leaves
2 tsp coriander seeds
2 tsp yellow mustard seeds
2 tsp cumin seeds
2 tsp ground turmeric
1 Tbsp masala spice
½ cup brown sugar
2 Tbsp apricot jam
1½ cups white vinegar
1 Tbsp cornflour dissolved in ¾ cup cold water
1kg fried fish pieces or fish balls

Heat oil in a pan and sauté the onions, ginger, garlic and chillies for about 2 minutes (not too long as the onions should have a slight crunch). Add the remaining spices and cook for a further few minutes. Stir in the sugar, apricot jam and vinegar, then slowly add the cornflour dissolved in cold water, stirring all the time until the sauce thickens and the sugar has dissolved.

Place a layer of the fish into a glass dish, followed by some sauce. Repeat until you've used all the fish and sauce. Refrigerate until ready to serve.

SERVES 4–6

The famous annual 'Sardine Run' off the southern coast of KwaZulu-Natal is a mass migration of sardines (or pilchards) during the winter months. The shoals are often more than 7km in length, 1.5km wide and 30m deep. Can you imagine being a scuba diver, snorkeller or even watching from the air? Pilchards are a daily protein in millions of homes in South Africa. This is a wonderful combination of a South African staple in the form of *kunkletten* (Yiddish for 'cutlets') served with a cooling, contrasting raita sauce. Soya yoghurt or mayonnaise could be used in the raita for a non-dairy alternative.

Gefilte PILCHARD FISH CAKES

1 onion, finely chopped or grated
3 Tbsp oil
1 x 490g can pilchards in tomato sauce (e.g. Lucky Star or Glenryck)
2 tsp curry powder
1 tsp finely grated fresh ginger
½ tsp crushed garlic
2 Tbsp finely chopped fresh coriander or parsley
1 cup breadcrumbs or matzah meal
1 egg, lightly beaten
salt and pepper to taste
oil for frying

Raita sauce

1 English cucumber, finely grated
1 cup full-cream yoghurt or mayonnaise for a non-dairy option
salt and pepper to taste

First make the raita by squeezing excess juice from the cucumber before combining it with the yoghurt or mayonnaise, salt and pepper.

To prepare the fish cakes, fry the onion in the oil, then transfer to a bowl and add the pilchards. Mash together or pulse in a food processor. Add the curry powder, ginger, garlic, coriander or parsley, breadcrumbs, egg, and salt and pepper, then mix well. Shape the mixture into balls and flatten slightly. Fry the fish cakes in hot oil until golden-brown. Remember that the fish is 'cooked' already so it shouldn't take too long.

MAKES 10–12

Bobotie is a popular South African dish of curried minced meat baked with a rich savoury custard. This recipe is prepared with fish, but non-dairy substitutes for the milk can be used for a ground beef version. The blintzes (crêpes) can also be made with dairy-free options, as well as potato flour instead of cake flour for a gluten-free version.

Bobotie FISH BLINTZES

Blintzes

3 extra-large eggs
1½ cups milk (or 1 cup soya milk and ½ cup water)
1 cup cake flour (or potato flour)
½ tsp salt

Fish bobotie filling

3 slices bread, crusts removed
1 cup milk (or soya or coconut milk)
1 large onion, finely chopped
3 Tbsp butter
½ tsp crushed garlic
2 tsp curry powder
½ tsp ground turmeric
2 Tbsp tomato paste
1 Tbsp smooth apricot jam
3 x 120g cans tuna in brine, drained
salt and pepper to taste

Topping

2 eggs
1 cup fresh cream (or non-dairy substitute)
1 cup milk or soya milk
a pinch of salt
2–3 bay leaves
a sprinkling grated nutmeg

Although blintzes are available from most supermarkets, I prefer to make my own. To make them, blend all the ingredients together in a food processor or mixer. Leave the batter to rest in the refrigerator for about 30 minutes; this allows the bubbles to subside and prevents the blintzes from breaking up. If using potato flour, refrigerating the batter is unnecessary as potato flour settles at the bottom and needs to be whisked before each blintz is made.

Heat a 20cm, non-stick frying pan over a medium to high heat, then gently pour a quarter to a third of a cup of the batter into the centre of the pan and swirl to spread evenly. Cook for about 30 seconds, flip it over (you can even lift and turn over with your fingers!) and cook for another 10 seconds. Repeat until all the batter has been used, layering the blintzes on top of one another or separating them with baking paper or plastic sheets.

For the bobotie filling, place the slices of bread in a bowl, pour the milk over them and leave to soak. Meanwhile, in a pan, fry the onion in the butter. As the onions start to soften, add the garlic, curry powder, turmeric, tomato paste and apricot jam and fry for another minute until well incorporated. Remove from the heat. Add the drained tuna and mix well.

Squeeze some of the milk out of the bread, then add the bread to the tuna mixture. Season with salt and pepper, and mix.

Preheat the oven to 180°C and grease a 20 x 30cm baking dish.

Start filling the blintzes with two tablespoons of tuna mixture each, folding the sides into the middle and rolling them up. Arrange them in the prepared baking dish.

To make the topping, beat the eggs, cream, milk and salt together, then pour over the filled blintzes. Place the bay leaves on top of the custard mixture, sprinkle with nutmeg and bake for 30 minutes.

MAKES 12–14

Latkes are one of the most famous Jewish foods, especially around Chanukkah when fried foods are traditional. There are a great many recipes for *latkes* and they can be served as appetisers, as a side dish, or even for tea with a sprinkling of confectioner's sugar. They are at their best straight out of the pan. Somehow mine never make it to the table and are eaten straight from the kitchen paper while still draining! This is my savoury version – delicious with chakalaka sauce or, as here, with a caper, parsley and aïoli sauce. If you prefer, you could substitute the snoek with salmon.

SMOKED SNOEK MOUSSE LATKES with a caper, parsley & aïoli sauce

250g deboned and skinned smoked snoek (or smoked salmon offcuts)
250g plain cream cheese (or non-dairy cream cheese*)

Latkes
3 large potatoes
salt and pepper to taste
½ cup cake flour or potato flour
1 egg
vegetable oil for frying

Caper, parsley and aïoli sauce
1 Tbsp capers, drained
1 tsp sugar
3 Tbsp finely chopped fresh parsley
½ cup mayonnaise
½ tsp crushed garlic

For the snoek mousse, purée the snoek (or smoked salmon) with the cream cheese (or substitute) in a food processor until smooth. Transfer the mousse to another bowl, cover with clingfilm and refrigerate.

To prepare the *latkes*, grate the potatoes, then wring out as much water from them as possible with a muslin cloth. Place in a bowl, season with salt and pepper, then add the flour and egg. Mix well. Place some of the potato in the palm of your hand and shape it into a little 'bird's nest'. Spoon a tablespoon of the fish mixture into the centre. Cover the 'nest' with more potato and compact it lightly. Repeat with the remaining potato and fish mixture.

Once all the *latkes* have been made, gently lower them into a pan of hot oil. If you have a deep-fryer, set it to 375°C. Fry until golden-brown and cooked through (approximately 4–5 minutes). Drain on paper towel and serve warm with the sauce.

To make the sauce, combine all the ingredients until well blended.

*If you can't find non-dairy cream cheese, you could mix 1 cup of whipped non-dairy creamer with 1 tablespoon of lemon juice.

MAKES 8

SECRET SAUCES

When I see the word 'secret' in association with a recipe, I almost feel as though I've knocked onto the door of a private club, only to be quickly ushered into their closet kitchen where covert operations are bubbling away on their stoves! A 'clove and kitchen dagger' scene, where nobody else is allowed to see the recipe but you! What fun it is to marvel over the mysteries of the 'secret' recipe! And why not? Isn't that just what cooking is all about? Using the basics – like everyone else – but secretly adding another of your favourite ingredients to the pot, to make it something extraordinary.

This can be made a few days ahead of time, and I usually double up on the quantities as it keeps so well.

MONKEY GLAND SAUCE

oil for frying
2 cups finely chopped onions
¾ cup sugar
¾ cup red wine (e.g. merlot)
1 tsp crushed fresh garlic
1 hot red chilli, chopped
1 Tbsp finely grated fresh ginger
1 cup finely chopped ripe red tomatoes
1 cup peeled and grated Granny Smith apples
1 cup tomato sauce or ketchup
1 cup chutney
2 Tbsp red wine vinegar or 2 Tbsp lemon juice

Heat a little oil and fry the onions until they are light brown. Add the sugar and continue to stir for a few minutes until they are caramelised. Pour in the wine and bring to the boil, stirring all the while, then reduce to a simmer. Add the garlic, chilli, ginger, tomato, apple, tomato sauce or ketchup, chutney and vinegar or lemon juice.

Bring the sauce to the boil, stirring all the time, then reduce to a simmer. Cover and leave to simmer for 5–10 minutes. Remove the sauce from the heat and blend with a hand blender or in a food processor until smooth.

MAKES 2 LITRES

RED WINE SAUCE for steaks

2 large onions, halved and sliced
3 Tbsp olive oil
salt and pepper to taste
1 tsp crushed fresh garlic
1 tsp dried origanum
2 Tbsp tomato paste
2½ cups dry red wine
2 Tbsp butter or non-dairy margarine

In a saucepan over a medium-high heat, cook the onion in the oil for about 5 minutes. Season with salt and pepper, then add the garlic and origanum and cook for another minute to release the flavours. Stir in the tomato paste and cook for 1 minute, then add the wine and simmer for 10 minutes or until it reduces by half to a lovely sauce. Strain the sauce and finally add the butter or non-dairy margarine.

This can be made beforehand. As you remove steaks from the pan to allow them to rest, add a cup of this sauce to the pan in which you were frying the steaks and scrape up all the meaty bits off the bottom of the pan. Bring to a low simmer. Just before you serve the steaks, cover them in this wonderful red wine gravy.

MAKES 1½–2 CUPS

For the greatest curry ever. If you add a spoon or two of this paste to your curry, you'll never have a bland, stewy, 'not so great' curry ever again.

MASALA PASTE

2 tsp mustard seeds
1 tsp cumin seeds
1 tsp coriander seeds
1 tsp fennel seeds
3 Tbsp cooking oil
4 fresh red chillies, seeded and roughly chopped
8 cloves garlic, roughly chopped
5cm piece fresh ginger, grated
2 tsp coarsely ground black peppercorns
1 tsp cayenne pepper
1 tsp ground cinnamon
1 Tbsp paprika
2 tsp garam masala
1½ tsp salt
¼ cup malt vinegar
2 Tbsp tomato paste
40g fresh coriander, roughly chopped
juice of 1 lemon
2 Tbsp ground almonds
¼ cup water

Fry the mustard, cumin, coriander and fennel seeds in the oil over a medium heat for 2–3 minutes to bring out the natural oils in the seeds. Add the chillies, garlic and ginger and continue to cook over a low heat for another 2 minutes. Remove from the heat and add the rest of the ingredients. Place into a food processor or use a hand blender to combine to a smooth paste.

Transfer the mixture to a glass jar with a tight-fitting lid and refrigerate. It should store well for at least 1 month. Remember to turn it over every so often to prevent any mould growth.

MAKES 1½ CUPS

This is the perfect herbalicious sauce for any meat. My favourite is a steak roll with the sauce spread over both inner sides of the bread roll.

Green CHIMICHURRI SAUCE

8 cloves garlic
30–35g fresh flat-leaf parsley
30–35g fresh coriander
20–25g fresh mint
20–25g fresh origanum
1 fresh hot green chilli (or more if you like it extra hot)
¼ cup white wine vinegar
½ cup canola oil

Place all the ingredients into a food processor and blend until smooth.

MAKES 1 CUP

Red CHIMICHURRI SALSA

1 red onion, roughly chopped
1 small red pepper, seeded and roughly chopped
5 cloves garlic, chopped
¼ cup red wine vinegar
2 red plum tomatoes, seeded and roughly chopped
2 Tbsp tomato paste
2 fresh small hot red chillies, chopped, or 1 tsp dried chilli flakes
1 tsp smoked paprika
1 cup fresh flat-leaf parsley
1 tsp dried origanum
½ cup olive oil
salt and crushed black pepper to taste

Combine all the ingredients in a food processor and pulse until well mixed. It must not be too smooth and should have a bit of texture.

MAKES 1½ CUPS

This triple dose of red jam is wonderful on just about anything. The combination of flavours will keep tasters guessing for as long as it took to make it! And that's quite a while! But that's what a chutney or jam is all about, an infusion of ingredients that need time to mingle and become something greater than the sum of their parts.

TOMATO KONFYT (triple red jam)

2 Tbsp olive oil
3 red onions, peeled and chopped
3 hot red chillies, chopped (or more if you want to spice things up!)
6 red peppers, seeded and chopped
1.5kg ripe tomatoes (cover with boiling water, then skin, chop and deseed) or 2 x 840g cans whole peeled Italian tomatoes.
1 large Granny Smith apple, cored, peeled and chopped
5cm piece fresh ginger, roughly chopped
2 bay leaves
1 tsp ground cumin
½ tsp ground cloves
2 cups sugar
½ cup red wine vinegar
salt and pepper to taste

Heat the oil in a pan and fry the onions, chillies and red peppers until just soft (but do not let them burn). Add the tomatoes, apple, ginger, bay leaves, cumin, cloves and sugar and stir well. Pour in the vinegar and bring to the boil, stirring all the time.

Once boiling, reduce the heat to low and allow the jam to simmer with the lid lying loosely on top to avoid any splattering, for 1 hour, stirring every so often to avoid any burning from sugar sticking to the bottom of the pan. Continue simmering in this manner, checking every 15 minutes, until it starts to reduce and darken in colour. A good test is to put a plate in the freezer, take it out and put a spoonful of jam on the plate. If it thickens and doesn't drip off the plate when turned sideways, it should be ready.

Set aside to cool, taste and adjust the seasoning if necessary. Store in a sterilised jar.

MAKES 3–4 CUPS

The Wife's
MUSTARD SAUCE

1 Tbsp mustard powder
1 Tbsp prepared, grainy mustard
2 Tbsp readymade 'hotdog' mustard sauce (e.g. All Joy or Heinz)
1 Tbsp brown sugar
3 Tbsp cornflour
a pinch salt
1 cup cold water
½ cup mayonnaise
1 cup non-dairy creamer
3 bay leaves

In a saucepan, combine the mustard powder, prepared mustard, hot dog mustard sauce, sugar, cornflour, salt and cold water, and mix well. Add the mayonnaise and creamer, then mix well. Switch on the heat and bring to the boil while whisking all the time. Once it has thickened, add the bay leaves and stir. Switch off the heat and allow it to absorb all the lovely flavours.

When ready to serve, reheat and discard the bay leaves.

MAKES 2–2½ CUPS

The Wife's
PERI-PERI SAUCE

1 large onion, roughly chopped
1 red bell pepper, deseeded and roughly chopped
4 Tbsp olive oil
1 bulb garlic, cloves peeled and roughly chopped
1½ cups African bird's eye chillies, stems removed
2 Tbsp tomato paste
juice of 2 lemons
1/3 cup red wine vinegar
1 Tbsp smoked paprika
3 heaped Tbsp soft brown sugar
2 bay leaves
1 Tbsp salt
1 tsp cracked black pepper
½ cup cooking oil

I like to bring the hearty flavours of this sauce out by first frying the onion and red pepper in the olive oil. I find it also helps the sauce to keep for longer.

Add the garlic, chillies, tomato paste, lemon juice, vinegar, paprika and sugar and stir well to mix. Allow to simmer for 5 minutes, then switch off the heat. Use a hand blender to blend until smooth. Add the bay leaves, salt and pepper, then add the cooking oil.

Transfer to a sterilised bottle, seal and refrigerate. Every third day or so, invert the bottle. This helps to prevent any mould from forming.

MAKES 2–3½ CUPS

Chakalaka is a spiced African vegetable relish, usually enjoyed as an accompaniment to *mieliepap*, boerewors, braaied meat, stews, on bread and with fish. Although often made with baked beans, this recipe doesn't include beans, probably because somebody in the family didn't eat beans when I first started making it. It yields quite a large batch, but as it lasts so long, there's no harm in going large! Don't forget to have sufficient sterilised glass jars ready.

CHAKALAKA

3 Tbsp sunflower oil
4 onions, finely chopped
2 tsp medium-strength curry powder
1½ tsp ground cumin
1 stalk celery, finely chopped
3 small green peppers, finely sliced lengthwise
2 green or red chillies, deseeded and finely chopped (or more, to taste)
4 cloves garlic, crushed
4 carrots, grated
2 Tbsp grated fresh ginger
6 large, very ripe red tomatoes
salt and black pepper to taste
1 tsp vinegar
1 tsp sugar or equivalent sweetener
½ cup finely chopped fresh parsley or coriander

Heat the oil in a pan and fry the onions until soft. Mix in the curry powder and cumin. Add the celery, green peppers, chillies, garlic, carrots, ginger and tomatoes, and mix well. Allow to boil for 15–20 minutes until the vegetables are soft. Finally, add the salt and pepper, vinegar, sugar or sweetener and parsley or coriander, and give it a good stir.

Decant into the prepared jars when cool.

MAKES 4 CUPS

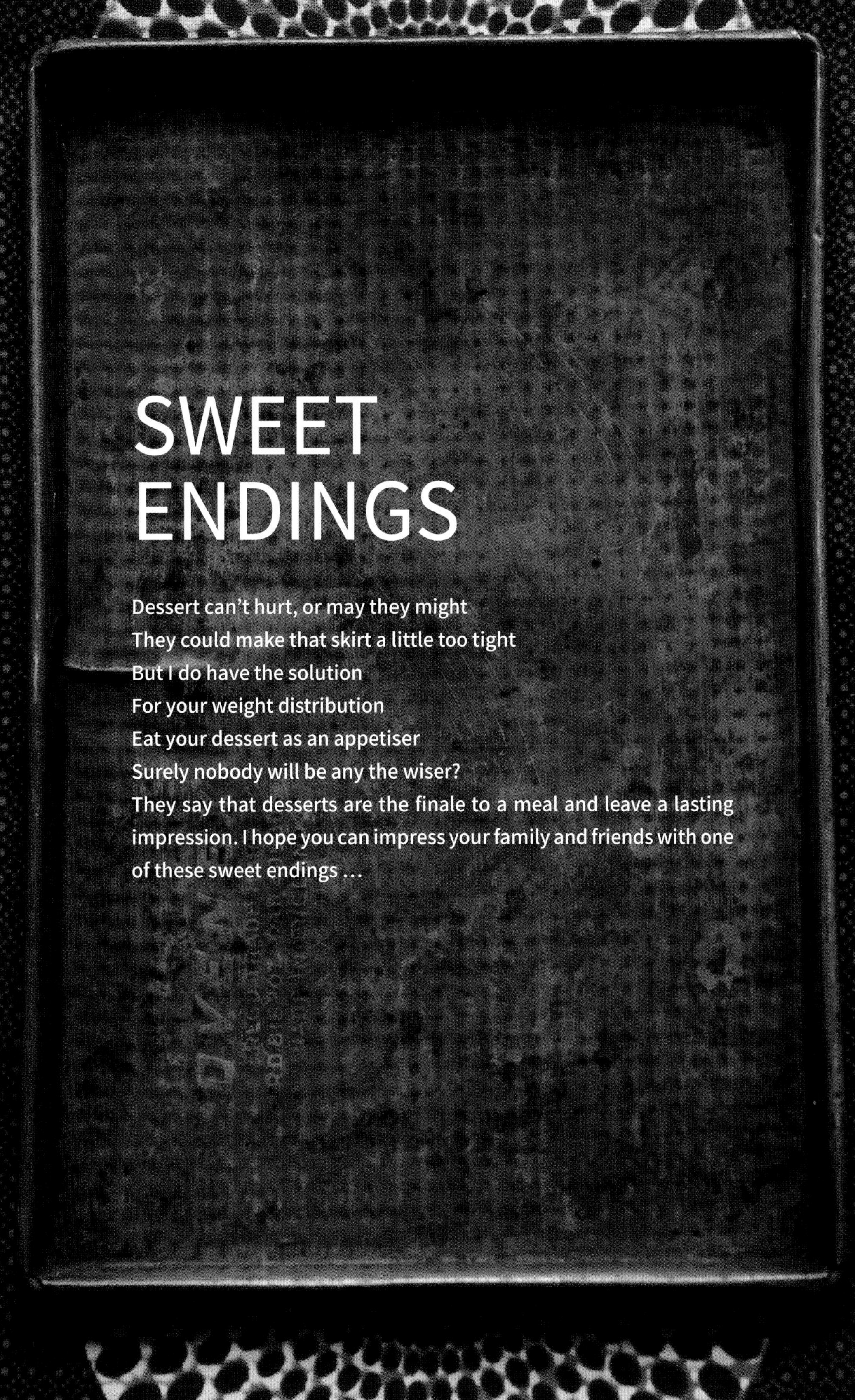

SWEET ENDINGS

Dessert can't hurt, or may they might
They could make that skirt a little too tight
But I do have the solution
For your weight distribution
Eat your dessert as an appetiser
Surely nobody will be any the wiser?

They say that desserts are the finale to a meal and leave a lasting impression. I hope you can impress your family and friends with one of these sweet endings …

Many South African commuters leave very early in the morning to get to work on time. Breakfast therefore becomes 'breakfast on the run' in some homes. The first time I saw these scones being made was when my domestic helper asked if she could make them for a family funeral she was attending and needed a large oven to make a sufficient quantity. They weren't the kind of scones my mother used to bake, which reached epic heights with the rich taste of butter, a spoonful of jam and lashings of cream. Rather, these scones served a purpose, to fill the tummies of the guests who had travelled many hours to pay their last respects. If the scones were a day or two past peak freshness, there was always a welcome cup of tea in which to dunk them.

AMAKHEKHE (township scones)

- 2 cups cake flour
- 200g sugar
- 2 tsp baking powder
- a pinch salt
- 1 cup butter, cut into pieces (or coconut oil at room temperature)
- 2 eggs, lightly beaten (or if you prefer firmer scones, use only 1 egg)
- ½ cup milk or coconut milk
- a handful seedless raisins (optional)
- 3 Tbsp smooth apricot jam dissolved in ½ cup boiling water
- 3 Tbsp brown sugar
- 2 tsp ground cinnamon

Preheat the oven to 180°C. Lightly oil a 12-cup muffin pan.

In a mixing bowl, combine the flour, sugar, baking powder and salt. Stir until well mixed. Using your fingers, rub the butter or coconut oil into the mixture until it resembles fine breadcrumbs. Lightly beat the eggs and milk together, then add to the mixture until a soft dough forms. If using, add the raisins at this stage and don't overwork the dough. Tip the dough out onto a well-floured surface and gently push or roll it out to about 3cm thickness.

Place spoonfuls of the dough into the cups of the prepared muffin pan. I like to bake them in a muffin pan as the dough is quite soft and the pan encourages a muffin shape. If you prefer the scones to have a firmer texture, add a little more flour to the mixture and cut the scones out with a biscuit cutter. For an authentic township touch, use a small jam tin to cut the scones out of the dough and place them 3cm apart on a baking tray.

Paint each scone with the dissolved apricot jam and sprinkle with brown sugar and cinnamon. Bake for 20 minutes until lightly brown.

MAKES 12

My grandchildren asked me to make them a *melktert* (milk tart), South Africa's all-time favourite. Naturally, I couldn't wait to get home and start baking. After cleaning out my storage shed I found recipe files and books going back 35 years. The page for this recipe was torn, but there was a handwritten note on top that stated 'outstanding recipe'. What a find of hidden treasures that day proved to be. Best of all, the *melktert* was just in time for Shavuot when we traditionally eat milk-based dishes. If you're making a non-dairy version, ensure that the biscuits are dairy-free too.

Bobba Shar's NO-BAKE MELKTERT

Base

200–250g tea biscuits, Nuttikrusts or Tennis biscuits, crushed
150g butter or margarine, melted

Filling

4 cups milk
3 Tbsp butter or margarine
1 x 395g can condensed milk
a pinch salt
1 heaped Tbsp custard powder
3 Tbsp cornflour
3 eggs, lightly beaten
2 tsp vanilla essence
ground cinnamon for sprinkling

First make the base. Place the crushed biscuits into a bowl, then add the melted butter and mix well. Press the mixture onto the base and sides of a pie dish with a 1.5-litre capacity. Refrigerate until ready to use.

In a saucepan, heat 3 cups of the milk, reserving the remaining cup to use later. Add the butter or margarine and condensed milk and keep stirring with a whisk. Just as it starts to come to the boil, remove from the heat and set aside to cool slightly.

Meanwhile, combine the salt, custard powder, cornflour and beaten eggs with the reserved cup of milk. Whisk until smooth. Very slowly add the cooled milk mixture to the egg mixture (it mustn't scramble the eggs) and keep whisking until well combined. Return this mixture to the saucepan in which the milk was warmed earlier. Heat and continue whisking until it thickens. (It's important to whisk all the time as the mixture must be very smooth, without any lumps. If you find a few, strain the mixture through a fine sieve.) Finally, add the vanilla essence and stir well.

Pour the filling into the refrigerated pie crust. Sprinkle with cinnamon and allow to cool. Cover with clingfilm and leave to set overnight.

SERVES 10

Bouquet Froze
ROSE SORBET

- 400g fresh strawberries, hulled and halved
- ½ cup sugar
- ¼ cup water
- 1 bottle rosé wine

Place the strawberries in a saucepan and add the sugar and water. Bring to the boil then reduce the heat and allow to simmer for another 2–3 minutes. Remove from the heat and leave to cool.

When cool, pour the wine over the strawberries and blend with a hand blender, food processor or liquidiser until smooth. Freeze for at least 6 hours. Blend the semi-frozen mixture until smooth and refreeze. The more you do this the smoother the sorbet will be.

Remove from the freezer 20 minutes before serving.

SERVES 6

If you've enjoyed Cape Town during the summer holidays, you must remember the ice-lolly vendors who have a unique way of selling their wares with their mantra, 'lolly for your dolly'. Granadilla juice can be replaced with orange juice.

GRANADILLA LOLLIES for the dollies

- 1 cup water
- 1 cup sugar
- 2 cups fresh granadilla juice
- 1 cup granadilla pulp

In a saucepan, bring the water and sugar to a boil for 10 minutes. Remove from the heat and slowly add the granadilla juice, then stir in the granadilla pulp. Pour the mixture into little 100ml plastic cups, cover with clingfilm and place a wooden sucker stick in the middle of each cup. Freeze.

MAKES 10–12

My first experience of baking, at almost seven years of age, was from a book called *The Singing Kettle*, edited by Selma Brodie. My reading was still very rudimentary, and our domestic helper at the time, who wanted to prove to my mother that she could bake, couldn't read either. I was oblivious to the harsh realities of the apartheid system at that age, but here was a lady, 33 years my senior, depending on me to read out the ingredients list while she drew pictures to remind herself of the recipe. This developed into a pattern: I read, she drew, and she baked while I went off to play. This two-way reciprocal relationship helped her to receive acknowledgement as a skilled baker and I was only too happy to be a skilled taster. It was also a real lesson proving that forced lack of education couldn't remove passion or motivation.

Beauty's TOFFEE NUT BARS

Bottom layer
125g butter
½ cup brown sugar
1 cup sifted cake flour

Topping
2 eggs, lightly beaten
1 cup brown sugar
3 Tbsp cake flour
1 tsp baking powder
1 tsp vanilla essence
½ tsp salt
1 cup desiccated coconut
200g flaked almonds

Options
jam of your choice
1 tsp ground cinnamon

To prepare the bottom layer, preheat the oven to 180°C. Have a Swiss roll tin at the ready, but do not grease it.

Beat the butter and sugar together, then stir in the flour. Use a knife to spread the mixture over the base of the ungreased tin. Bake for 10–15 minutes until golden-brown. Remove from the oven and leave to cool until just slightly warm.

In a bowl, mix together all the topping ingredients. Use a wooden spoon to spread the mixture over the slightly warm bottom layer. Return to the oven and bake for another 25 minutes until the topping is golden-brown. Leave to cool slightly, then cut into squares.

If you'd like a few alternatives, you could spread a layer of jam over the bottom layer before covering with the topping, or you could add the cinnamon to the topping mixture.

MAKES 20–25

Everybody has their 'best cheesecake recipe ever'. Whether you're adding a couple of extras such as apples, strawberries or chocolate to a basic recipe, the basic ingredients have to be there. After experimenting with cheesecake recipes for many years, I still hold onto my mother's basic recipe as 'The Best', and to that I've added a couple of twists here and there for a decadent look and taste. Here's her basic recipe with the addition of apples and a streusel topping, or if you're in the mood for something really decadent, try the optional decorative topping.

BOBBA'S CHEESECAKE
with caramel-apples & streusel topping

1 box Nuttikrust biscuits or your favourite tea biscuits
150g butter, melted
3 extra-large eggs
¾ cup sugar
3 x 250g tubs full-cream cream cheese
½ cup sour cream
¼ cup cake flour
1 tsp vanilla essence
1 tsp lemon juice
1 x 495g can pie apples
2 tsp ground cinnamon
3 Tbsp brown sugar

Streusel topping
1 cup brown sugar
½ cup cake flour
a pinch salt
3 Tbsp butter
1 Tbsp ground cinnamon

Decorative topping (option)*
1 large Granny Smith apple, peeled, cored and very thinly sliced
1 Tbsp butter
2 Tbsp syrup
3 Tbsp fresh cream

Crush the biscuits in a food processor (or with a rolling pin), then mix with the melted butter until smooth. Line the base of a spring-form cake tin with the mixture and refrigerate while preparing the filling and topping.

In the bowl of a food processor or mixer, beat the eggs and sugar together until light and creamy. Reduce the speed and slowly add the cream cheese, sour cream, flour, vanilla essence and lemon juice until well blended. Do not overbeat at this stage as it may cause the top to crack.

Pour half of the mixture over the cold biscuit base. Delicately place the pie apples over the cream-cheese mixture and sprinkle with the cinnamon and brown sugar. Cover the apples with the remaining cream-cheese mixture.

Preheat the oven to 180°C.

Combine the topping ingredients, then crumble the mixture with the tips of your fingers. Sprinkle the mixture over the top of the unbaked cheesecake.

Bake, uncovered, for 25 minutes, then reduce the temperature to 160°C and bake for another 20 minutes. Switch the oven off and leave the cheesecake inside for a further 15 minutes. If necessary, place a sheet of aluminium foil on the cheesecake after the first 25 minutes – if the streusel is golden-brown already – but continue to bake at the lower heat as the cheesecake still has to cook through the middle.

Remove from the oven and allow the cake to cool completely in the tin. Before removing from the tin, run a knife between the outer edge of the cake and the inside of the tin. Position the cake on a serving dish and carefully release the spring.

*If you're opting for something more decadent, fry the Granny Smith apple in the butter and syrup until soft and the liquid has turned to caramel. Add the cream and leave it to simmer for another 2 minutes. Just before serving the cake, pour the mixture over the top.

SERVES 8

This dessert or fridge tart has been voted in the top ten of favourite South African puddings for over 50 years. I've tried to make a non-dairy version, but somehow, like cheesecake, it's at its best when dairy. What more can I say? Indulge!

PEPPERMINT CRISP FRIDGE TART

2 x packets Tennis biscuits
1 x 380g can Nestlé Caramel Treat (original)
2 cups fresh cream, lightly whipped
250g peppermint crisp chocolate, grated (or more)1 x 380g can Nestlé Caramel Treat (peppermint flavour)

Grease a 30 x 15cm tart dish.

Arrange a layer of biscuits in the base of the dish. Mix together the original Caramel Treat and cream and spoon a 1cm-deep layer over the biscuits. Sprinkle a third of the peppermint crisp chocolate on top of the caramel layer. Follow this with another layer of biscuits. Spread a layer of the peppermint Caramel Treat over the biscuits, followed by peppermint crisp chocolate. Repeat for another 2 layers or until all the ingredients are used, ending with a caramel layer topped with peppermint crisp chocolate. Refrigerate for at least 4 hours (but preferably overnight) before serving.

SERVES 8–10

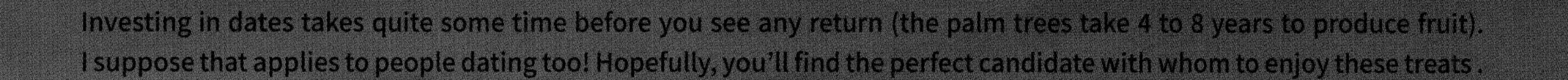

Investing in dates takes quite some time before you see any return (the palm trees take 4 to 8 years to produce fruit). I suppose that applies to people dating too! Hopefully, you'll find the perfect candidate with whom to enjoy these treats .

UPDATED BALLS

250g butter or margarine
1 cup treacle or muscovado sugar
500g pitted dates
1 packet Marie biscuits or tea biscuits, roughly crushed
1 cup Rice Krispies
1 tsp vanilla essence
1½ cups desiccated coconut, toasted
2 Tbsp syrup
1 cup crushed pecan nuts

In a saucepan, melt the butter or margarine and sugar together over a low heat. Add the dates and allow them to soften over a medium heat for about 5 minutes until well blended. Add the biscuits and Rice Krispies, vanilla essence, 1 cup of the coconut, the syrup and pecan nuts. When cool enough to handle, shape the mixture into balls, then roll them in the remaining coconut until well coated.

MAKES 18–20

Ystervarkies are small cubes of cake that are dipped in chocolate sauce and then rolled in coconut, to resemble hedgehogs (*ystervarkie* is the Afrikaans word for 'porcupine'). If you're like me, you don't have the patience to make Lamingtons, even though they're delicious and worth the *patshke* (fuss) to make, try my shortcut version. It's equally delicious and not so messy. To keep it dairy-free, substitute milk in the cakes with coconut milk, and butter with oil.

YSTERVARKIES (Lamington cake)

Sponge cake

1 box vanilla cake mix, prepared as per box instructions
1 box red velvet cake mix, prepared as per box instructions

Syrup

1½ cups castor sugar
2 cups boiling water
1½ Tbsp butter or non-dairy margarine
½ tsp vanilla essence
a pinch salt
200g Lindt or good-quality dark chocolate, chopped

Frosting (icing topping)

2 cups sifted icing sugar
2 Tbsp butter or non-dairy margarine
1–2 Tbsp boiling water
200g desiccated coconut

Bake both the vanilla and red velvet cakes in rectangular or square baking tins of the same size. Turn the cakes out and leave to cool completely. When cool, slice each cake horizontally through the centre to create 2 layers of vanilla cake and 2 layers of red velvet cake.

Make the syrup by heating the sugar and water together. Add the butter or margarine, vanilla and salt. Add the chocolate and allow to melt, stirring until smooth. Reduce the heat to very low – sufficient to keep the chocolate sauce warm, but not hot.

Place one of the vanilla cake layers onto a plate and evenly pour a quarter of the chocolate sauce over this layer. Position a layer of red velvet cake on top of the vanilla, then pour over another quarter of the chocolate sauce. Repeat with the remaining cake layers.

To make the frosting, combine the icing sugar, butter or margarine and boiling water and mix until smooth (you may need to add another tablespoon of boiling water, as long as the mixture can spread easily). Cover the entire surface of the 4-layer cake with the frosting and sprinkle with a generous layer of desiccated coconut. If the coconut falls off, dip the icing palette into boiling water and spread a little moisture over the icing before re-applying the coconut. Slice into squares.

MAKES 20–30 SQUARES

These are an old-fashioned favourite, called 'crunchies' by most South Africans. Although a favourite from way-back-when, they can now benefit from so many of the new seeds available on the market, so here's my version of these healthy treats.

OATIES
with lots of seedies

2 cups rolled oats (e.g. Jungle Oats)
½ muscovado sugar
1 cup desiccated coconut
½ cup sunflower seeds
½ cup chia seeds
½ cup sesame seeds
2 cups Rice Krispies
a pinch salt
1 cup melted butter or ¾ cup coconut oil
1 cup syrup or honey
½ tsp bicarbonate of soda

Preheat the oven to 180°C. Line a baking tray 24 x 36 x 1cm and lightly spray with cooking spray.

In a bowl, combine the oats, sugar, coconut, all seeds, Rice Krispies and salt. Heat the butter (or oil) and syrup together, then stir in the bicarbonate of soda. Pour this into the oat mixture and stir well to mix. The mixture should be glossy and visibly well coated.

Press into the prepared baking tray and bake for 25 minutes. Switch the oven off but leave in the tray for another 10 minutes. Mark into squares, then cut and turn out of the tray onto a cooling rack to cool.

These should become more crisp as they cool, but still be soft enough to bite into. If you would like them a bit firmer, return them to the oven at 160°C, on the cooling rack, and bake for another 5–10 minutes.

MAKES 25–30

Tired of making *teiglach* that stick to the *tseyna* (teeth) and don't let go until they've taken hold of a crown or even a double row of false teeth? I've seen that before! This Rosh Hashanah, when it's symbolic to eat something sweet, why not try a soft, delicious koeksister? A koeksister looks like a tiny challah, but it's fried until soft in the centre and crispy on the outside, then immediately immersed in syrup.

As a nation, we're accustomed to the melting pot of cultures and traditions that have been passed down through our colourful history. One that stands out above the rest is our love of all things sweet. Who can say no to a sticky koeksister dripping with syrup? This is the recipe for the Afrikaans version of koeksisters. A variation of the sweet treat is the traditional Cape Malay 'koesister' where the 'k' is dropped in the spelling, the shape is different, the taste is slightly spicier, the dough is softer, and it's rolled in coconut.

TEIGLACH VS KOEKSISTERS

500g cake flour
2 level Tbsp baking powder
60g margarine or cold coconut oil
1 large egg, beaten
1 cup water
sunflower oil for frying

Syrup
2 cups water
1kg sugar
1 tsp cream of tartar
2 Tbsp lemon juice
4–5cm piece fresh ginger
1 stick cinnamon

First prepare the syrup. In a saucepan, bring the water, sugar and cream of tartar to the boil. Once it starts to boil, add the lemon juice, ginger and cinnamon, then continue to simmer for 10 minutes. Leave the syrup to cool to room temperature, then pour half into a bowl and place over ice to cool rapidly. Place the remaining syrup in the fridge to cool.

To make the dough, sift the flour and baking powder together in a bowl and then rub in the margarine or cold coconut oil with your fingertips. Add the beaten egg to the water and whisk to combine. Make a well in the centre of the flour mixture and pour in the egg mixture. Gradually mix until a smooth dough has formed. Knead thoroughly. Cover with clingfilm and leave to rest for at least 15 minutes or up to 5 hours.

Pour oil into a frying pan to a depth of about 10cm and heat to 160 °C.

Using an oiled rolling pin, roll out the dough on an oiled surface to a thickness of 5mm. Cut the dough into rectangles of 6 x 15cm. Cut each rectangle lengthways into 3 strips, leaving one side uncut. Plait the 3 strips and press the cut ends together firmly.

Fry in batches of 6 in the hot oil for 6–7 minutes, or until dark golden-brown. Drain them for a few seconds on kitchen paper. Be careful not to let the oil become too hot as the koeksisters will burn on the outside, but will still be raw inside. Equally, if the oil is too cold, the dough will just soak it up and become soggy. Cover the raw koeksisters with a damp cloth to prevent them from drying out while frying the others.

Dip the fried koeksisters into the ice-cold syrup while they are still hot. Remove from the syrup with a slotted spoon and place on a wire rack. The syrup will gradually become hot with use, so once you have dipped about half of the koeksisters, continue dipping in the remaining syrup in the fridge.

Brush the koeksisters with more syrup when they are completely cooled, to look very shiny and beautiful when you serve them to your friends!

MAKES 12–14

'Klippies' is the nickname of the well-known Klipdrift brand of brandy in South Africa. A firm favourite at many a bar and around the braai, brandy-and-coke or Klippies-and-coke is the twist in this oh-so South African moist, syrupy pudding.

Brandy (Klippies) and Coke MALVA PUDDING

1 cup cola
½ cup water
250g pitted dates, chopped
1 tsp bicarbonate of soda
1 cup coconut oil
1 cup soft brown sugar
2 Tbsp apricot jam
2 large eggs
2 cups cake flour
1 tsp baking powder
½ tsp salt
1 tsp ground cinnamon
1 tsp ground ginger
grated peel of 1 orange
1 cup chopped pecan nuts
½ cup desiccated coconut

Brandy syrup
½ cup soft brown sugar
⅓ cup syrup
½ cup dairy or non-dairy creamer
½ cup water
1 tsp vanilla essence
¼ cup brandy

Preheat the oven to 180°C. Grease a rectangular (± 25 x 35cm) or oval-shaped baking dish.

In a saucepan, pour the cola and water over the dates and bring to the boil. Remove from the heat, stir in the bicarbonate of soda, then leave to cool.

In a bowl, beat the coconut oil, sugar and apricot jam until well combined. Add the eggs, one at a time, and continue to beat. Add the flour, baking powder, salt, cooled dates and liquid, cinnamon, ginger, grated orange peel, pecan nuts and coconut, and mix until well combined, but not overmixed. Transfer the mixture to the prepared dish and bake for 50 minutes.

Meanwhile, make the syrup by combining all the ingredients in a saucepan over a medium heat until the sugar has dissolved.

Pour the warm syrup over the pudding as it comes out of the oven. Poke holes all over the top and run a knife around the edge of the pudding so that all the syrup soaks in.

Serve with vanilla ice cream or custard.

SERVES 8–10

Carrots are one of the major vegetables consumed in South Africa. Yes, it is difficult to encourage some people to eat them, but if they're hidden well enough, as in this cake, or disguised in orange and apple juice with a hint of ginger, they should get their dose of beta-carotene.

My brother swears that my gluten-free carrot cake is better than my regular one that uses cake flour. This cake is moist, tasty, tropical and healthy. If you don't have all of these flours in your cupboard, you could use two-and-a-half cups of gluten-free cake mix, but I love the nutty taste of the almond flour and the wonderful taste of the coconut flour that goes so well with the pineapple. I like to serve this cake at Rosh Hashanah (New Year) because the Yiddish word for carrots, *meren*, also means 'to increase'. Carrots symbolise the hope that we will increase our good deeds in the coming year.

Gluten-free, Dairy-free CARROT CAKE

½ cup psyllium husk
½ cup brown rice flour
½ cup tapioca flour
½ cup almond flour
½ cup coconut flour
4 eggs
1 cup brown sugar
1 tsp vanilla essence
¾ cup coconut oil
¾ cup sunflower oil
2 tsp ground cinnamon
½ tsp ground ginger
½ tsp ground mixed spice
1 x 490g can crushed pineapple, drained (optional)
3 cups finely grated carrots
1 cup crimson or regular seedless raisins
100g pecan nuts, roughly crushed
1 tsp bicarbonate of soda
2 tsp baking powder
a pinch salt

Non-dairy cream cheese icing*
3 cups icing sugar, sifted
125g non-dairy cream cheese (e.g. Tofutti), or ¼ cup non-dairy creamer mixed with 2 Tbsp lemon juice

Preheat the oven to 180°C. Grease 3 round cake tins with a diameter of 22cm.

In a bowl, sift and combine the psyllium and all the flours together.

Beat the eggs, sugar and vanilla essence together in a food processor for about 5 minutes until well mixed. Slowly add the coconut and sunflower oils and continue beating for another 2–3 minutes. Switch off the processor and add the flour mixture, cinnamon, ginger, mixed spice and pineapple (if using). Switch the processor on to a low speed and blend until just combined. Fold in the carrots, raisins, nuts, bicarbonate of soda, baking powder and salt.

Divide the mixture among the 3 cake tins and bake for 40–45 minutes.

While the cake is baking, make the icing by mixing the icing sugar and cream cheese together until smooth, but don't add all the cream cheese at once as it may become too runny. It should be a firmish, spreadable icing.

When the cake is cool, sandwich together and ice with the icing.

*If you are making this *milchik* (dairy), you can use icing sugar and regular cream cheese.

SERVES 8–12

Mandelbrodt (almond bread) in Yiddish, rusks in South Africa, biscotti in Italy ... whatever you call them, remember they have to be twice-baked to ensure that hard, crunchy bite. South Africans have been dunking rusks since the days of the Voortrekkers, and speaking of *treks*, there isn't a trip that I make without a box of rusks in my suitcase! Whether it's making rusks out of leftover bread, *babke* or bagels, nothing need go to waste when a rusk is an option.

VANILLA HEALTH RUSKS with buttermilk

1 x 600g packet vanilla cake mix
2 cups All-Bran flakes
1 cup rolled oats
½ cup sunflower seeds
1 cup chopped almonds or pecans
250g butter
½ cup canola or coconut oil
2 cups buttermilk
2 extra-large eggs, at room temperature

Adjust the oven shelf to the middle position. Preheat the oven to 180°C. Line the base of a 35 x 24 x 4cm baking tin with baking paper.

Toss the cake mix, All-Bran flakes, oats, sunflower seeds and nuts together in a large mixing bowl.

Melt the butter in the microwave in a 1-litre glass measuring jug. Add the oil and buttermilk and mix well. Beat in the eggs. Pour over the dry mixture in the bowl and (using a spatula) stir everything together until well blended. Do not overmix. Scoop the mixture into the prepared baking tin and smooth down to level.

Bake for 45 minutes. While still warm, cut the rusks into singles. Freeze them overnight (still in the baking tin). The following day, remove the rusks from the baking tin and arrange them on a metal cooling rack or baking sheet (leaving space between each rusk). Return them to the oven and bake at 120°C, allowing them to dry out for 2–3 hours.

Leave to cool down completely before storing in an airtight container.

MAKES 15–20

RECIPE INDEX